# GETTING BETTER
# BIT(E) BY BIT(E)

# Getting Better Bit(e) by Bit(e)

## A Survival Kit for Sufferers of Bulimia Nervosa and Binge Eating Disorders

### Ulrike Schmidt

*and*

### Janet Treasure

*Institute of Psychiatry*
*London, UK*

Routledge
Taylor & Francis Group

LONDON AND NEW YORK

Psychology Press Ltd, Publishers
27 Church Road, Hove, East Sussex BN3 2FA
711 Third Avenue, New York, NY 10017 (8th Floor)

*Routledge is an imprint of the Taylor & Francis Group, an Informa business*

**British Library Cataloguing in Publication Data**
A catalogue record for this book is available from the British Library

ISBN 978-0-86377-322-8

Printed and bound in the UK by TJ International Ltd, Padstow, Cornwall
This publication has been produced with paper manufactured to strict
environmental standards and with pulp derived from sustainable forests.

# Acknowledgements

Our special thanks go to Tom Treasure, who contributed the cartoons. Jane Tiller kindly supplied us with some of the case vignettes. Dave Attwell, Kate Trotter, Becky Trowler, and Nick Troop made helpful comments on the manuscript. We gratefully acknowledge the help of Janice May in preparing the manuscript.

This work was undertaken when we were working in the Eating Disorders Unit of the Maudsley Hospital, led by Professor Gerald Russell.

All royalties from this book will go to the Mental Health Foundation and the Eating Disorders Association.

Last, but not least, we would like to acknowledge our patients, many of whose comments and ideas were invaluable in developing this book.

# Contents

# Introduction

Although the media are now taking a great interest in eating disorders, perhaps this interest has served more to glamorise bulimic disorders than to inform about them. There still seems to be a great deal of mystique surrounding the problem, and there are many misconceptions and much misinformation about what causes bulimia, what the health risks are, and how the problem can be overcome. Access to treatment is still very difficult for sufferers living in many parts of the country, and their friends and relatives often feel completely in the dark as to what to do to help. Some doctors are not very sympathetic to sufferers, enhancing their sense of guilt and loneliness.

This book was originally written for the bulimic patients attending the Eating Disorder Clinic at the Maudsley Hospital. Many of the patients we see need basic information about the various aspects of their difficulty and simple practical advice on how to overcome the problem. The psychotherapy programmes run by our unit and by other eating disorder clinics in this country attempt to address these issues. This book contains in condensed form what we know to be the essential ingredients of treatment. The book has now been given to a large number of eating disorder patients attending our clinic, and we have been very encouraged by their response. Many of them, upon reading it, felt empowered to tackle their eating problem and, beyond that, to address other difficulties in their lives too. Other patients—often those who were less sure about what they wanted—felt that the book did help them to understand their problems better and has given them the tools to make an informed decision about whether or not to enter treatment.

This book could help you, too, to make the journey to recovery and act as your guide. You must undertake the journey of change yourself, but we hope to provide maps and to point out the dangers and pitfalls along the route.

You may have mixed feelings about leaving the security of the familiar territory of bulimia nervosa. Although you know that there are severe dangers on all sides, you may have constructed a smoke screen which keeps the dangers out of sight. You will be frightened about entering the new territory where there may be no comfort or protection. This book is filled with the travellers' tales of people like yourself who have made the journey before you. Many of our patients have contributed to this book. We have recorded their stories and their suffering to help decrease your sense of isolation.

This book will help you avoid the snares that self-defeating thought patterns will throw up to catch you. It contains the tools needed to make the journey and travel along the road to recovery. It will show you changes that you can make so that the short-lived rewards that you get from bulimia are replaced by better, more long-lasting alternatives.

With this book you should be able to anticipate, and be prepared for, holdups and detours on the way. You may have some initial discomfort (for example, any new exercise will produce transient aches as new muscle groups are brought into use), but eventually you will recognise the benefits of your new-found strengths.

Not everyone is able to make the trip successfully the first time. Setbacks and relapses commonly occur. However, you will be able to learn from your setbacks and relapses. For some sufferers, the change process is slow and laborious, and it takes many attempts before the goal is attained; others will find that the way is easier.

People differ in how long the journey to recovery should take. Three months is the average, but it is often necessary to consult the maps or guides at intervals over a few years to ensure that strong currents have not returned you to bulimia nervosa once more.

You may feel "I can't help myself. I have tried. My problem is too severe for this. I need someone else to take over." Any form of treatment can only work if you are actively involved. The more you put in, the more you will get out of it. So you might as well make a start now. However, we don't expect that anything that you read in this book will suddenly make you "snap out of your problem". By making a decision to stop your chaotic eating pattern, you will have taken the important first step on a journey that leads to increased freedom and increased self-esteem.

## A FEW WORDS OF CAUTION

A number of people are persuaded by their families or partners to work on their problems. This book can only help you if YOU really want to get better for YOURSELF. It can't help if you are not ready to change, or if you just want to change for somebody else's sake. To assess this you need to go to chapter 1 and fill in your own balance sheet and then keep it with you (in your bag or pocket) for regular consultation wherever you go.

You will be asked to embark on a lot of hard work over the next few weeks. Even if you are very determined to get better, there are bound to be ups and downs. The best way to deal with this is to take each day as it comes and not to dwell on the past.

You may feel a temptation to "binge" on this book, i.e. to read it quickly and to throw it into a corner, and tell yourself you knew it all already. If you are honest to yourself, that is probably not true. Try to digest each chapter slowly.

## WHAT THIS BOOK CAN AND CAN'T DO

This book can't cure you. However, the book can help you to get much better, so that the eating disorder doesn't rule your life any more. The book is not aimed primarily at helping you to understand why you developed an eating problem. Understanding the underlying causes is often difficult and only happens very gradually, in some cases it may be impossible. Although understanding what caused the eating problem is important, it does not often in itself help to change distressing eating symptoms. This book is aimed at helping people to improve their symptoms and to gain some control over their lives. Once eating symptoms have improved, the underlying causes often become a lot clearer, and it is much more possible to decide then whether they need treatment in their own right.

## FURTHER READING

Abraham, S., & Llewellyn-Jones, D. (1992). *Eating disorders—The facts*. Oxford: Oxford Medical Publications.

Buckroyd, J. (1989). *Eating your heart out. The emotional meaning of eating disorders*. London: MacDonald Optima.

Dana, M., & Lawrence, M. (1989). *Women's secret disorder. A new understanding of bulimia*. London: Grafton Books.

Duker, M., & Slade, R. (1990). *Anorexia and bulimia—How to help*. Milton Keynes: Open University Press.

French, B. (1987). *Coping with bulimia. The binge-purge syndrome*. Wellingborough: Thorsons Publishing Group.

Hollis, J. (1985). *Fat is a family affair. A guide for people with eating disorders and those who love them.* Center City, MN:Hazelden.

Lawrence, M. (ed.) (1987). *Fed Up and Hungry.* London: Women's Press.

Melville, J. (1983). *The ABC of eating. Coping with anorexia, bulimia and compulsive eating.* London: Sheldon Press.

Orbach, S. (1978). *Fat is a feminist issue.* London: Hamlyn Paperbacks.

Orbach, S. (1984). *Fat is a feminist issue 2.* London: Hamlyn Paperbacks.

Roche, L. (1984). *Glutton for punishment. A personal story of the bingeing/starving syndrome.* London: Pan Books.

Singh, J., & Rosier, P. (1990). *No body's perfect. Dealing with food problems.* Dublin: Attic Handbooks.

# CHAPTER ONE

# The Way Forward

## DO I SUFFER FROM BULIMIA?

There is a bewildering number of labels that acknowledge that a person has a problem with overeating and is distressed about it. You may have come across some of them: compulsive overeating, bulimia nervosa, bulimia, binge eating disorder, or bulimarexia. These labels overlap and have an awful lot in common with each other. Problems with overeating can occur in people of any body weight (skinny, average, and overweight). This book has been written for people who fall into any of these categories. If you are unsure whether any of this fits you, fill in and score the test in Table 1.1.

If your severity index score is 5 points or above, it is very likely that you have a significant eating disorder at present.

If your symptom score is 15 points or above, you have a lot of the thoughts and attitudes that go with an eating disorder and are clearly distressed by it.

## HOW TO USE THIS BOOK

Like many people, you may have the habit of starting books at the end or in the middle, perhaps flicking through the pages and beginning with a chapter with a particularly catching title. In principle there is nothing to stop you doing that with this book, but there are a few things that you need to know before you make a start: Chapters 1 to 6 are the core

TABLE 1.1

Bulimic Investigatory Test, Edinburgh

| Questions | Scores |
|---|---|
| 1. Do you have a regular daily eating pattern? Yes = 0, No = 1 | ___ |
| 2. Are you a strict dieter? Yes = 1, No = 0 | ___ |
| 3. Do you feel a failure if you break your diet once? Yes = 1, No = 0 | ___ |
| 4. Do you count the calories of everything you eat, even when not on a diet? Yes = 1, No = 0 | ___ |
| 5. Do you ever fast for a whole day? Yes = 1, No = 0 | ___ |
| 6. If yes, how often is this? Have once = 1; now and then = 2; once a week = 3; 2–3 times a week = 4; every second day = 5 | ___ |
| 7. Do you do any of the following to help you lose weight? (a) Take diet pills; (b) Take diuretics (water tablets); (c) Take laxatives; (d) Make yourself vomit. Never = 0; occasionally = 2; once a week = 3; 2–3 times a week = 4; daily = 5; 2–3 times a day = 6; 5+ times a day = 7. Answer questions 7 (a)–(d) separately, then add them all up. | ___ |
| 8. Does you pattern of eating severely disrupt your life? Yes = 1, No = 0 | ___ |
| 9. Would you say that food dominated your life? Yes = 1, No = 0 | ___ |
| 10. Do you ever eat and eat until you are stopped by physical discomfort? Yes = 1, No = 0 | ___ |
| 11. Are there times when all you think about is food? Yes = 1, No = 0 | ___ |
| 12. Do you eat sensibly in front of others and make up in private? Yes = 1, No = 0 | ___ |
| 13. Can you always stop eating when you want to? Yes = 0, No = 1 | ___ |
| 14. Do you experience overpowering urges to eat and eat and eat? Yes = 1, No = 0 | ___ |
| 15. When you are feeling anxious do you tend to eat a lot? Yes = 1, No = 0 | ___ |
| 16. Does the thought of becoming fat terrify you? Yes = 1, No = 0 | ___ |
| 17. Do you ever eat large amounts of food rapidly (not a meal)? Yes = 1, No = 0 | ___ |
| 18. Are you ashamed of your eating habits? Yes = 1, No = 0 | ___ |
| 19. Do you worry that you have no control over how much you eat? Yes = 1, No = 0 | ___ |
| 20. Do you turn to food for comfort? Yes = 1, No = 0 | ___ |

*(Continued)*

TABLE 1.1 *(Continued)*
Bulimic Investigatory Test, Edinburgh

| Questions | Scores |
|---|---|
| 21. Are you able to leave food on the plate at the end of a meal? Yes = 0, No = 1 | ___ |
| 22. Do you deceive other people about how much you eat? Yes = 1, No = 0 | ___ |
| 23. Does how hungry you feel determine how much you eat? Yes = 0, No = 1 | ___ |
| 24. Do you ever binge on large amounts of food? Yes = 1, No = 0 | ___ |
| 25. If yes, do such binges leave you feeling miserable? Yes = 1, No = 0 | ___ |
| 26. If you do binge, is this only when you are alone? Yes = 1, No = 0 | ___ |
| 27. If you do binge, how often is this? Hardly ever = 1; once a month = 2; once a week = 3; 2–3 times a week = 4; daily = 5; 2–3 times a day = 6 | ___ |
| 28. Would you go to great lengths to satisfy an urge to binge? Yes = 1, No = 0 | ___ |
| 29. If you overeat do you feel very guilty? Yes = 1, No = 0 | ___ |
| 30. Do you ever eat in secret? Yes = 1, No = 0 | ___ |
| 31. Are your eating habits what you would consider to be normal? Yes = 0, No = 1 | ___ |
| 32. Would you consider yourself to be a compulsive eater? Yes = 1, No = 0 | ___ |
| 33. Does your weight fluctuate by more than 5 pounds in a week? Yes = 1, No = 0 | ___ |
| *Adding up and analysing the scores* | |
| Total for questions 6, 7 and 27. This will give you a severity index. | ___ |
| Total for all other questions. This will give you a symptom score. | ___ |

Adapted from M. Henderson & C.P.L. Freeman (1987). *British Journal of Psychiatry, 150,* 18–24. Reproduced with permission.

chapters that will teach you all the steps you need for cracking unhealthy eating habits. It is sensible to read chapters 1 to 6 together, but you can do this in whatever order you like. With the help of these chapters you will be able to decide whether you are correct in making the decision that you want to get over your bulimia and are ready to do so.

If in addition to a problem with your eating habits you are also overweight, you should include chapter 7 in your initial reading.

Chapters 8 to 14 focus on the links between your eating disorder and the rest of your life. You can read them at a leisurely pace over the next few weeks, in whatever order you like. The aim of these additional chapters is to help you spot problems in different areas of your life, to get you to make some connections with factors that may have contributed to the origins of your eating problem or are obstacles for overcoming it.

If you are currently drinking heavily or are regularly taking drugs, you should look at chapter 12 early on. Drug and alcohol problems make your eating difficulty much more difficult to control and should therefore be tackled early on. Chapter 12 will help you (a) to assess how serious your alcohol/drug problem is, and (b) to decide what to do about it.

## FIRST STEPS

### Are You Ready to Undertake the Journey?

Before starting, it is important to dip into the core chapters (2–6) of the book to obtain basic background information.

Read chapters 2, 3, 4, 5, & 6 Now. Don't attempt to follow any of the instructions given there, skip over these. Re-read each chapter until you are sure that you have been able to take the information on board. Are you ready to undertake the journey?

• Now, when you have a quiet hour, work on writing your bulimia balance sheet.

First, take a large sheet of paper and divide it length-wise into two main columns. At the top of one column write, "Reasons for giving up bulimia", and on the other write, "Reasons for staying bulimic". You may have important reasons to fear change from familiar behaviour, and yet part of you is desperate to shake yourself out of the vicious circle that is keeping your bulimia nervosa going. It is impossible to keep all these thoughts and ideas together in your head at one time as our memory has its limits, and so there is a tendency to swing from one side of an argument to the other. Writing a balance sheet will help you to deal with all of your thoughts systematically. Plan to work on this project during a week—keep going back to it each day.

In order to focus your thoughts, make four divisions across the sheet and at the start of each row, write:

1. Practical gains and losses for SELF
2. Practical gains and losses for OTHERS
3. Emotional gains and losses for SELF (self-approval or self-disapproval)
4. Emotional gains and losses for OTHERS (social approval or disapproval)

Here are examples from the balance sheets of others, which may help to get you started. You may agree with some of the comments and want to add them to your list. But give yourself time to find your own reasons, and make them as specific as possible. Have this balance sheet in the back of your mind all week, so that new ideas can pop up unexpectedly when you are doing something else.

*Reasons to Give up Bulimia*
1. *Practical gains to self*
   "I won't be tired and unwell all the time."
   "My teeth won't continue to be destroyed."
   "I will look healthier."
   "My guts will work normally without unnatural practices."
   "My body will begin to repair the damage I have caused."
2. *Practical gains for others*
   "I will be able to spend more time with my family and friends and will not have to make excuses to avoid eating with them."
   "My flatmates won't find the food cupboards empty."
   "I will be more romantically/sexually responsive."
   "My partner will be able to kiss me if I no longer vomit."
   "I will be less irritable and snappy."
   "I will be able to concentrate and do a better job at work."
3. *Self-approval*
   "I won't have to lie about food and how much I eat."
   "I won't have to deceive people about vomiting and taking laxatives."
   "I will have achieved something positive."
4. *Social approval*
   "My parents will stop worrying that I will die."
   "My friends won't have to see me destroying my life."
   "My parents/husband/boyfriend will no longer have to suffer the shame of being associated with someone suffering from an obvious psychiatric disorder."
   "At work I will appear healthy and competent."
   "I will be able to join in all social activities without excuses."

*Disadvantages of Change and Recovery*
1. *Practical loss to self*
   "I will find meal-times very frightening."
   "I will feel bloated and stuffed too full."
   "My stomach may 'blow out' after eating small amounts."
   "I may get some swelling around my eyes and ankles."
   "I will become very frightened about my weight."
2. *Practical loss to others*
   "I will need more active help and support from my parents/spouse."
   "My mood may swing more."

3. *Self-disapproval*
   "It will be so difficult that I'm bound to fail and then I will feel worse than ever."
   "I will feel out of control over everything."
   "I will have to face up to my responsibilities."
   "I will feel uncomfortable, miserable, and frightened."
   "I will hate myself and my body."
4. *Social disapproval*
   "I will no longer be able to let others think that I am controlled about eating and my weight."
   "I may become more assertive and dominant when relieved of this burden of shame and guilt, which may upset the status quo in my relationships."

Don't worry if you find it difficult to distinguish between these four categories, which have just been made to help focus your thoughts. There is quite a bit of overlap between them. It doesn't really matter which exact category you put any reason in, as long as it is in the correct column, i.e. positive or negative.

When your balance sheet is finished, go over the list and give each reason a rating on a 1–10 scale (10 = a very important reason; 1 = only slightly important reason).

## BACK TO THE FUTURE

We now suggest that you do the following exercise. You will find it helpful to have your balance sheet in front of you while you do it.

Imagine yourself in five years' time, after you had decided that it was too difficult and risky to overcome your eating disorder. You continue to have bulimia nervosa. Everything has gone wrong. All the negative consequences that you considered in your balance sheet have come true. You feel at the end of your tether. You decide to write to your one close friend, whom you haven't seen for a while as she (assuming your friend is a woman) has been abroad. You know that she cares about you and will not be deceived by superficial news and that when you meet her on her return she will see it all anyway. You have found in the past that she has been able to provide emotional and practical support when you have needed help. You know that you can, and must, give her a full account of your present difficulties.

*Here Are a Few Guidelines for You to Consider.*
- What weight will you be?
- What medical complications will you have?
- What career/job will you be pursuing?

- Where and with whom will you be living?
- Who will be your friends?
- Will you be in a relationship? married? have children?

Now be as realistic as possible, and talk in the present tense. Here is an example of a letter from another sufferer from bulimia nervosa, who is preparing herself to undertake the journey of recovery:

*25th May 1998*

*Dear Susan,*

*I am looking forward to seeing you again in June. I thought I should be open with you about my current situation so that we can pick up where we left off when you arrive back. I'm afraid it's rather a sad story, but I know I can trust you with it, and I even have faith that something good will come out of it, as happened in the past.*

*My bulimia has continued, which means I have had it for 15 years now. My weight has fluctuated greatly between 8 and 13 stone. At the moment I am just over 8 stone, but I remain unhappy.*

*I continue to vomit, although it doesn't seem to be as effective as it once did, and I now severely restrict my food. I spend all day preparing my food. I keep a semblance of control by wrapping small bites in dried seaweed. In the morning I sometimes wake to find that I have eaten at night but cannot remember it. The illness has taken a severe toll on my health. I now have six caps on my teeth, and the others remain very sensitive to temperature changes. Last summer I was in hospital in agonizing pain with kidney stones. I had special new vibration treatment to disperse them. I passed blood and gravel in my urine for weeks afterwards.*

*I'm more hooked on laxatives than ever before. I spend all day walking to chemists' shops to buy them. I have a fixed routine and visit different shops on different days of the week. I spend more than half my social security money on laxatives. I have found that the amount I need gradually increases. Without laxatives I become so bloated and bunged up that I am terrified, and yet with them I bleed and leak and am up all night on the toilet.*

*I have not worked for the past two years. I rent a room in a house with six others. Since David finished with me four years ago, my social life has shrunk. I only remain in contact with Sophie and Paul. They write to me regularly and come and pick me up to take me to their house. At times I feel so low and so full of despair that I contemplate ending my suffering. I hold back as I am a coward and also because I couldn't bear to think of people seeing my room or belongings after I am dead. I would be ashamed for them to see my hoards of food (I have 3 deep freezers filled with food) and my hoard of trinkets, which I have stolen from shops and never used. The compulsion to collect and clean is overwhelming.*

*Despite all of this, I do have a glimmer of hope. I remember that five years ago you offered to help me overcome my illness. It seemed too difficult and risky then to change. However, I now see that there is no other way forward, and I would like to accept that offer of help that you so generously made before.*

*I know that you will be pleased that I have made this first step and have written to you.*

*With love from Penny*

- Now write your own letter. Read it through very carefully. Do you really want a future like this?
- Refer back to the guidelines at the start of this section. Now write a second letter. Imagine your situation in five years. This time you have successfully controlled your bulimia. Is this the sort of future you want to aim for?

## MAKING YOUR DECISION TO GO

Whether you decide now to work at change or to continue with bulimia nervosa will result from a decision made by you. It will probably not be simply a question of one decision but of numerous smaller decisions that you will make over the following days, months, and years. There will be strong forces sucking you back. You will make many mistakes; after all, you are human and fallible. However, being human, you can also learn from your mistakes.

### Should I Involve Someone to Help Me?

Trying to get better on your own is a hard and a lonely task. In some cases it is useful to enlist the help of family or friends. Sometimes your family may be keener on the idea of helping you than you are to have them help you. If you are unsure whether to involve your family or friends, you should look at chapter 13, which will help you clarify whether it might be a positive step for you to involve them in your treatment, how to involve them in the best way, and whether you are asking them for the right reasons. You will need to decide whom you will ask to give you support. Will it be people you are closest to or those that you spend most time with?

The questions outlined in Table 1.2 may help you in making a decision.

TABLE 1.2

Support Questionnaire

| Could person X be your support? Answer the following questions: | Score |
|---|---|
| 1. How easy is it to talk to X about your problem?<br>Very easy (5 points); quite easy (4 points); Not sure (3 points);<br>quite difficult (2 points); very difficult (1 point) | —— |
| 2. Is X critical or easily upset about your eating?<br>Always (1 point); often (2 points); sometimes (3 points); rarely (4 points);<br>never (5 points) | —— |
| 3. Could you talk to X even if you weren't making progress?<br>Definitely (3 points); not sure (2 points); definitely not (1 point) | —— |
| 4. Can you trust X to be always there when you need someone—with no strings attached?<br>Definitely (5 points); probably (4 points); maybe (3 points);<br>probably not (2 points); definitely not (1 point) | —— |
| 5. If you overcame your bulimia, what would X's likely response be?<br>(a) X would feel quite threatened by this and feel redundant (0 points)<br>(b) X would feel jealous of me becoming more independent and successful with my life (0 points)<br>(b) I haven't a clue (1 point)<br>(b) X would be very pleased for me (2 points) | —— |
| 6. How often are you in contact with X?<br>At least once a week (3 points)<br>At least once every fortnight (2 points)<br>At least once a month (1 point)<br>Less than once a month (0 points) | —— |
| Total number of points | —— |

*Analysing your score*

19 to 23 points: You are in the lucky position of having a perfect supporter near you. You should definitely ask person X to help you in your efforts to overcome your eating disorder.

12 to 18 points: It is uncertain whether X should be your supporter. Maybe you don't know them well enough yet to be able to say what their response to you would be. Perhaps your best bet is to keep X in mind as a potential support, but not to rush into anything. However, if you do know X very well, your score may simply reflect that X is rather luke-warm about their commitment to you, and you may be better off thinking about someone else.

4 to 11 points: Look for someone else, or go it alone.

Asking for support will be difficult. Try to be as direct and as specific about what you want your potential supporter to do as possible. Perhaps you should give them this book to look at.

Helping someone with an eating problem is a difficult task. Some people may foresee these problems and decline to help early on. You should expect this. It is not rejection but realism. Others may take it on, wishing to please and help you without knowledge of the implications and then find it too difficult—you should expect this. Again, it is not rejection but realism.

If you are lucky, you may have one of those rare people around you, who will be able to help and stick with it. It will be difficult and treacherous for both of you, but the rewards are great. You will need to take an active part in defining the amount of support that will be helpful. Spend at least 15 minutes per week reviewing progress and setting new goals with your "co-therapist". You may want to show or share with your "co-therapist" some of the exercises we suggest in this book.

Trust will be a difficult issue. The secret life of a sufferer with an eating disorder leads to suspiciousness in others. You will need to discuss this with your supporter. Tell them that if they become suspicious or anxious, they should talk to you about it. Encourage them to state what has made them worried. They must try to be direct and present the facts, rather than carry out a character assassination or withdraw their help with "the hump". For example, they may need to say, "You've been working hard not to binge, and you have been able to join with me for several evenings. However, you ate very little at supper last night and appeared tense and rushed off so early. I'm wondering if you've started to binge and vomit again."

You may work with your supporter to think of ways to alter your behaviour when you get an urge to eat. For example, you may come home from a difficult day at work feeling tense and hopeless, with thoughts such as "I never do anything right" spinning in your head. Instead of bingeing, which would temporarily remove these thoughts, you may try to go out for a walk with your supporter to discuss together your thoughts and feelings and gain a different perspective.

An alternative form of support that may work for you might be to join the self-help meetings run by the Eating Disorders Association (address at the end of the book). Parents or concerned others often find these meetings helpful too, and can feel that they are doing something useful and yet are less intrusive.

Even if you decide to go it alone, it will be a good idea to set aside 30 minutes each week (or more frequently) for review. Try to use your diary as a friend and confidante. Perhaps use this time to write a letter as if to a "co-therapist", or paint yourself a picture or a collage summarising the week. End by marking goals into your diary for this week and evaluating progress of difficulties from the week before.

## HOW TO STAGE YOUR JOURNEY

Before you begin to work with this book (after you have browsed through it and done the introductory exercises), you must decide—perhaps with the help of your supporter—to set yourself realistic and manageable goals. It will be very overwhelming to state: "I am never going to binge again in my life." Such an over-keen, unrealistic goal can be a trigger for more binges! It helps if you break down your overall goals into more manageable steps. Chapters 2 to 6 will help you to get some idea of what goals might be realistic as starting points in order to overcome various aspects of your eating disorder. In trying to reach a goal, it is important to have an exact description of what you want. This must be in terms of:

1. Something that you can plan and do yourself.
2. It must be something that is measurable (not just something that is impossible to measure, such as happiness).
3. Goals should challenge you slightly, so that you will feel pleased when they are done, but not so impossible that only Wonder-woman alone could accomplish them.
4. Goals should be defined within a realistic time frame. Having no time limit leads to procrastination. Having a goal in which you state: "I will not do X for the rest of my life" is equally unhelpful, as you would only know that you had met your goal when you were dead.

Think of The Little Engine and The Hill. This small engine was able to conquer the hill by saying:

"I think I can, I'm sure I can,
I think I can, I'm sure I can".

CHAPTER TWO

# Tools for the Journey

## HOW TO KEEP A THERAPEUTIC DIARY

Have a look at the sample diary page at the back of this book. If you have access to a photocopier, why not just copy it? You can then carry a single diary sheet around with you every day, and collect all the sheets in a folder. If you don't have access to a photocopier, you will have to make up your own diary. Buy a booklet small enough to fit into your pockets or a bag. The ground rules for keeping a diary are simple:

- The diary is to help you as a friend would. It is not meant to be a persecuting "spy in the cab".
- For every day, write down what you have eaten and drunk. Try to be as accurate as you can.
- Write down those occasions when you should have eaten or drunk but avoided it.
- Always keep your diary with you. Take it with you even to the loo. Record even things you find shameful and embarrassing.
- Record things when they are happening. That gives the clearest idea of what was going on at the time.
- Do not write a novel: try to find a "short-hand" way of describing what was happening at the time.
- Do not leave writing your diary till the end of the day, as this will make it very inaccurate.

Until you get into the habit of diary-keeping, you may want to break it down into stages. Get used to scribbling down what you eat for a week or two; thereafter move on to the ABC approach described below. The detective work then follows.

*"A" is for antecedents (triggers).* Write down:

- Where were you at the time of eating, and what was going on (i.e. were you on your own or in company, at home or at work, etc.)?
- What were your thoughts beforehand? Who said what?
- What were your feelings beforehand?

*"B" is for behaviour.* Write down:

- Whether you thought what you ate was a binge.
- Whether you were sick and how often.
- Whether you used laxatives or diuretics, and in what amounts.

*"C" is for consequences.* Write down:

- What were the consequences—both positive and negative—in both the short and long term upon your thoughts, feelings, and behaviour?

You can then build up the behaviour chain:

|  | thoughts |  | positive consequences |
|---|---|---|---|
| "A" |  | → "B" Behaviour → "C" |  |
|  | feelings |  | negative consequences |

The most difficult aspect of the detective work will be to become aware of your triggering thoughts and feelings. Chapter 10, "Food for Thought", describes the thinking traps that commonly occur with eating disorders. Most triggering thoughts and feelings are unpleasant, and you may prefer not to dwell on them, but the energy used to blot them out takes a long-term toll on well-being. Although these thoughts and feelings are not enjoyable, they are necessary and important signals that indicate that you may need to change some aspects of your life. In Table 2.1 we have included excerpts from a diary sheet completed by Anna, one of our patients, as an example.

Although this diary should only take a few minutes a day to complete, you are bound to find keeping it on a daily basis inconvenient at times, if not irritating. Start it on a day when you are not so busy that you are bound to fail to keep it. Keeping it for one or two days a week completely is better than one week of inaccuracies.

TABLE 2.1
Anna's Food Diary, Week 1 and Week 4

### Week 1

| Time | What eaten | B | V | L | Antecedents & Consequences |
|------|-----------|---|---|---|----------------------------|
| 8.00 | All-bran | | | | A: Still full from yesterday.<br>C: Must make an effort not to binge today. |
| 12.00 | 1 apple | | | | A: Hungry.<br>C: Still hungry, mustn't eat more in case it starts me off on a binge. |
| 3.00 | 1lb grapes, 2 choc. bars | | ! | | A: Had phone call from John, he would be home late.<br>C: Disgusted with myself. I am the most hopeless person in the world. |
| 6.00 | peanuts & chocolates, picked from shopping | !! | | | A: No food in flat. Had to go shopping. Couldn't stop myself putting loads of sweets in the trolley. Ate loads of stuff in the car. Had to go on eating once at home. |
| | | | !! | | |
| 7.00 | 2 portions of curry, 3 choc. bars | !! | !! | | C: Very angry with myself. I feel so lonely. Totally exhausted, went to bed early. |

### Week 4

| Time | What eaten | B | V | L | Antecedents & Consequences |
|------|-----------|---|---|---|----------------------------|
| 8.00 | Cottage cheese,2 sl. toast with honey | | | | Enjoyed this. |
| 11.00 | apple | | | | |
| 12.30 | baked potato, tuna fish | | | | Eaten in the canteen at work. Tina said: "You haven't been here for ages." Could have run away, felt everybody was looking at me. |
| 3.00 | yoghurt, crunch bar | | | | |
| 6.00 | 1 sl. of toast | | | | |
| 7.00 | fish & vegetables, 1 portion of ice cream | | | | Had not planned dessert. John suggested ice cream. My initial response was to say no, but I knew I would then finish the packet off whilst washing up. So I had a portion and enjoyed it sitting with John. John put it away and made coffee, which we drank relaxing on the settee. Washing up left. |

B = Binge, V = Vomited, L = Laxatives

We find that people vary greatly in their response to keeping this diary. You may be a person who loves writing diaries and who is able to treat it like a trusted, reliable friend in whom you have no difficulty confiding. Good. You will not have any difficulties with the approach used.

On the other hand, for a variety of reasons you may absolutely loathe keeping a diary. You may simply find it boring. Or you may find it very frightening and shameful and find it extremely hard to face up to what you are doing to yourself. You may also be worried about someone else finding the diary. Or perhaps you worry that it might make you worse to concentrate on your food intake so much. You may feel very tempted to stop writing your diary every time you have had a binge. Try to be as honest as you can. It must be said that getting over this problem will involve facing up to very frightening feelings, thoughts, and behaviour. Blocking these off will not help in the long term.

Some people find that simply keeping a diary helps them to regularise their eating habits and may lead to considerable improvement. For others it may not be that easy.

### Shula

Shula had severe anorexia nervosa. She spent a long time in hospital, and her weight increased to the level it had been before the onset of her illness. However, after discharge she was left with very painful, prolonged binges, which happened every day. She induced vomiting several times a day and took about 150 laxative pills a day. She kept her food diary religiously, as she felt it gave her some sense of being in control amidst all her chaos. After three or four months of keeping a diary (and trying to work on her eating problem), she felt that very little had changed, so why continue keeping it? Shula was asked to go over her diary again and to draw up a chart of the number of binges, episodes of vomiting, and number of laxatives taken per week (Figure 2.1).

To her surprise, she discovered that she had actually decreased all the features of her eating problem, most remarkably the laxatives, but that bingeing and vomiting were also reducing gradually. You may say, "How could she have failed to notice such a dramatic improvement?" Well, it's very easy when change is drawn out over a long period of time, and especially on a bad day, when everything looks gloomy to you. Shula decided to put up the weekly chart in her bedroom, to give her strength at times when she felt she wasn't changing.

No. of tablets
per week

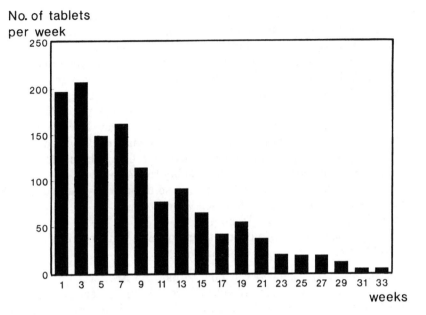

FIG. 2.1. Laxative chart.

## NEW SKILLS TO COPE WITH OLD DIFFICULTIES

You will find that, in gradually learning to give up retreating into the patterns of bulimia nervosa as a means of coping with life's difficulties, you will need to develop new skills.

### Learning to Solve Problems in Seven Steps

Making decisions and solving problems, small or large, is a definite skill. People vary in the ways they reach solutions for problems. Some do it just intuitively; it has to feel right emotionally or agree with certain "rules" that they live by. Others do it mainly by trying to find the most rational solution. There is no right or wrong way and we all use mixtures of these two approaches. The seven steps outlined below are guidelines which are useful to follow when you are trying to find a way of coping with life's demands and stresses without bulimia nervosa.

*Step 1:* What is the problem? This step may sound trivial, but you do need to define your problem carefully. Try to write one simple sentence putting your problem in a nutshell.

*Step 2:* Finding possible solutions. Many people get stuck because in trying to find a solution they limit themselves too early in the number of alternative solutions they consider. Put all constraints aside and try to find as many solutions as you can. Let your imagination run riot. Do not exclude anything just because it seems selfish, crazy, unrealistic, or far fetched. Jot down anything that comes into your mind.

*Step 3:* Looking at options in detail. For each solution you have found go through the pros and cons, even for those solutions that seem silly.

*Step 4:* Choosing a solution that fits you. By going through step 3 you should have a clearer sense of what is right or wrong for you. If you are still unsure what seems to be the best option, you may have to go back to step 2 and create more solutions, or you may not be ready to do anything about the problem you have defined. Can it be shelved for a while? What are the pros and cons of doing that?

*Step 5:* Finding ways of putting your solution into practice. Think through all the steps needed to reach your solution.

*Step 6:* Carry it out step by step.

*Step 7:* Check the final outcome to ensure that your solution has been a suitable one.

In chapter 1 we showed you how to use the first steps of problem solving to make the decision to get over your bulimia nervosa. You may want to read over your bulimia nervosa balance sheet now. In chapter 14 we discuss the use of problem solving in relation to career decisions. Here is an example which applies problem solving to relationships:

*Andrea*

Andrea's boyfriend, Ian, had recently split up with her. Shortly afterwards, Phil, one of her old boyfriends, began to ring her up daily and to visit her regularly. Her parents, who had greatly disliked Ian, supported this development. Her mother would repeatedly tell her how nice Phil was, and she would invite him round to their house without telling Andrea. Andrea was confused and upset about splitting up with Ian, she was angry about her mother's attempts to pair her off with Phil, and she was irritated, but also flattered, by Phil's attention. She felt that the pressure she was put under, both by her mother and by Phil, to go out with him was hard to resist and that she might end up giving in to it. After having been told about the problem-solving approach, Andrea defined her problem in terms of the seven steps:

*Step 1:* My problem is, I don't know what I want. Part of me knows I am not ready to enter a new relationship and that I need space and time to get over Ian, who hurt me really badly. Part of me feels that if my mother, whose judgement I trust in other things, approves of Phil, he must be good for me. And also, as he clearly cares so much about me, maybe I'd be a fool to reject him.

*Steps 2 and 3:* Andrea then wrote down the following possible solutions:

(a) To become Phil's girlfriend again. Pros: This would keep everyone happy, my feeling of being under pressure would ease, I would have someone to comfort me. Cons: In the long run I'd probably feel as discontented and bored as when I went out with Phil before.

(b) Never to see Phil again and put the phone down every time he rings. Pros: It would give me space and ease pressure. Cons: I would definitely lose a good friend.

(c) To avoid going home to see my parents till they have accepted that I don't want to be with Phil. Pros: Again, pressure would be reduced. Cons: I would miss my parents, I like going home, and I appreciate my mother's advice on most issues.

(d) To beg Ian to make a fresh start. Pros: If he took me back, I'd be unbelievably happy. Cons: If he said no to me, I'd feel even more hurt than I do now.

(e) To find myself another boyfriend. Pros: It would be like making a completely new start. Cons: Nice new boyfriends aren't all that easy to find. Moreover, at the moment I don't think I can feel anything for a new person.

(f) To run away to the South Pacific. Pros: I'd be away from all the misery, and all the new impressions would help me to get over my upset. Cons: I don't have the money. Travelling can be a lonely affair, especially when you are not feeling your best.

(g) To take an overdose and risk dying. Pros: It would make Ian realise how much he hurt me. Although it would probably not make him change his mind about finishing with me, I would have the grim satisfaction of knowing I had got back at him. It would really teach him a lesson. Cons: I am really scared of dying. I might seriously damage my health and end up as a brain-damaged vegetable. I would feel very ashamed after taking an overdose. It would hurt my parents, my sisters, and a number of friends who have all been very kind to me recently.

(h) To move house and go ex-directory, so that nobody can find me. Pros: It would definitely decrease hassle. Cons: I don't want to move house, and I need friends and support.

(i) To explain to my mother that, although I do appreciate her opinion on a lot of issues, I think on this occasion she is wrong in trying to make up my mind for me. To explain to Phil that I do not want to be his girlfriend, but I do want to remain his friend. Pros: I would continue to get support from both my mother and Phil. I would get the space to get over Ian. Cons: It might be quite difficult to talk to my mother and Phil, and there is the danger I will hurt them. I will still be left with a lot of sad feelings for Ian and won't have an instant relief from them.

*Step 4:* In considering her options more closely, Andrea realised that she didn't want to become Phil's girlfriend again, and she firmly rejected Option (a). She also rejected options (b), (c), (e), (f), (g), (h), which, she felt, all had an element of running away in them. This left her with two options: (d) and (i). She felt there was still a strong pull towards being back with her old boyfriend, Ian, and she therefore looked at this option in detail.

Option (d) was to beg Ian to make a new start. Pros: If he took me back, I'd be unbelievably happy. But would I really? I still would be left with all the hurt over how he told me he didn't want to see me any more and with the worry that he might decide to dump me again like a hot potato, as he did before. Cons: If he said no to me I would feel even more hurt than now. Could I actually stand it to be rejected by him again?

Andrea remained unsure whether or not to take up this option. She decided to shelve it for two weeks, and if, after that, she still wanted to contact Ian, she might.

She then considered Option (i). She thought: "There is nothing to stop me from getting on with that now. Whatever happens with Ian, I need to sort things out with my mother and Phil."

*Steps 5 and 6:* She decided to tackle Phil first, which, she knew, would be easier. She told him that she appreciated his friendship and would always do so, but that she felt he was looking for more than that from her. She told him she did not want to become his girlfriend again, especially as she still felt very cut up about Ian.

She knew she was going to find it difficult to talk to her mother, and, in preparation, she jotted down on a piece of paper what she wanted to say: "Mum, I need to talk to you about something that is bothering me. You know I am still pretty upset about Ian, and you have been a great help with listening to me so patiently. But there is one thing that is not helping. You keep inviting Phil round to cheer me up, but it just doesn't work. It would help me more if you stopped doing that." She considered how her mother might react to this. There was some risk that her mother would get very upset and cross. Andrea thought it would be crucial that she chose a good time for them to discuss the issue and that, even if her mother did get upset, she would not hold it against her for the rest of her life.

She waited until she and her mother were alone at home on a Saturday afternoon and both quite relaxed, and then she approached her. As she had predicted, her mother was very upset. She said that she had only wanted to help, that Andrea was accusing her of matchmaking, which she had never tried to do, and that in future she would leave Andrea to sort out her own problems. Andrea left her mother feeling quite shaken up but still convinced that she had done the right thing.

*Step 7:* Her mother did stop inviting Phil around and making references to him, and two weeks later she even apologised to Andrea for having tried to interfere in her life. Phil continued to ring Andrea frequently, but somehow their conversation had cleared the air, and she no longer felt so pressurised by his phone calls.

Andrea's example shows that often there is no neat solution to a problem and that, like Andrea, in choosing an option, you may choose some risks and problems too.

## FURTHER READING

Honey, P. (1983). *Solving your personal problems.* London: Sheldon Press.

# CHAPTER THREE

# Dieting: A Health Warning

## BEAUTY IS IN THE EYE OF THE BEHOLDER

What is considered to be the ideal female form has varied over time. Fashion thrives on change. What will be the preferred female body shape in five years' time? At any point in time, only a tiny minority of women will fit in with what is considered to be a fashionable shape.

*Rosamund*

Rosamund, a 17-year-old budding ballerina, was told by her principal that her technique and presentation were excellent, but that she had a problem—her breasts were too large. She was advised to consider plastic surgery to reduce their size. She was very upset by this report. She wanted eventually to marry and have children. Would this mutilation for the sake of her art interfere with this? Dieting seemed the only answer. She restricted her intake severely, but bulimia quickly developed, and her weight increased rather than fell.

These powerful messages and drastic remedies do not just affect women.

*Stephen*

Stephen, a builder, lost a foot in a car accident. He became interested in health and fitness and went to the gym to train regularly. Friends there suggested that he use steroids to build up his muscles. He did, but his family and girlfriend became concerned about the change in his personality. He became more irritable and lost his temper at the slightest provocation. One day, whilst driving, he became enraged when overtaken by another car. He set off in pursuit, despite his girlfriend's protests. She died in the resulting car crash.

Several examples of murders committed by men taking anabolic steroids have been reported.

The dangers, sacrifices, and mutilations to which people submit themselves for the sake of some ideal of beauty are astounding, especially when the goals are not shared with others. But perhaps this is part of human nature.

With the loss of beliefs in gods and fate, the whims and chances of nature are more and more considered to be under personal control. No longer do we say "she has all the luck", "the gods smiled on her". Any deviation from normality is blamed upon mistakes, neglect, and bad practices. You, too, can be beautiful if you only try hard enough or spend enough money and time on potions, practices, and surgery.

## WHAT WEIGHT IS HEALTHY?

Table 3.1 gives the weight ranges (for different heights) into which the majority of people fall. As with height and shoe size, there is a large range of weights that are healthy. Some people are heavier than others, just as some people have bigger feet. (The current fashion of slimness is

TABLE 3.1
The Weight Band that is Appropriate for Your Height

| Height (ft/ins) | Height (metres) | Weight (stone) | Weight (kg) |
|:---:|:---:|:---:|:---:|
| 5' 0" | 1.50 | 7st  2 to  8st 12 | 45–56 |
| 5' 1" | 1.52 | 7st  4 to  9st  2 | 46–58 |
| 5' 2" | 1.56 | 7st  8 to  9st  7 | 48–60 |
| 5' 3" | 1.58 | 7st 11 to  9st  9 | 49–61 |
| 5' 4" | 1.61 | 8st  1 to 10st  1 | 51–64 |
| 5' 5" | 1.63 | 8st  3 to 10st  3 | 52–65 |
| 5' 6" | 1.66 | 8st  7 to 10st 10 | 54–68 |
| 5' 7" | 1.68 | 8st 12 to 10st 13 | 56–69 |
| 5' 8" | 1.70 | 9st  2 to 11st  5 | 58–72 |
| 5' 9" | 1.73 | 9st  7 to 11st 11 | 60–75 |
| 5'10" | 1.75 | 9st  9 to 12st  2 | 61–77 |
| 5'11" | 1.77 | 10st    to 12st  7 | 63–79 |
| 6' 0" | 1.80 | 10st  1 to 12st  9 | 65–81 |

perhaps no stranger than the ancient fashion in China for women to have small feet. The crippling bandages are now replaced by diet strait-jackets). Extreme overweight and underweight is associated with ill health and a short life.

If your weight is above the weight band given for your height, you should have a look at chapter 7 which has been written specially for you.

## What Weight is Right for Me?

The weight and shape you are is determined mainly by your physical constitution. The genes you inherited, which programme your body, cannot be changed. To assess the weight and shape you may have inherited:

- Draw your family tree in your diary, and write in all the weights and heights of your family members.
- Collect photographs of your grandmothers, grandfathers, great-aunts, mother, father, aunts, and uncles when they were your age. Paste them in an album.

*Enid*

Enid came from a plump family; her mother, aunt, and grandmother had all been stout. She developed early and was bigger than all her school friends. She was ashamed when her periods began whilst she was at junior school. She started to diet when she read on the back of a packet of tights that her ideal weight was 2 stone below her current weight. She never reached that weight, because bulimia began.

If, like Enid, you come from a family in which most members are plump, it is likely that your healthy weight is at the top end of the normal range.

Muscles and bones are much denser than fat tissue. If you are an athlete, or the rest of your family have an athletic build, you should also expect your weight to be at the top end of the normal range. Similarly, if everyone in your family is big-boned, it is likely that you, too, should be at the top end of the normal range.

For many sufferers of bulimia, achieving a healthy weight simply means going back to the weight they were before their eating problems began. For some of you this message will be hard to swallow.

## Are Weight Fluctuations Normal?

A person's weight normally goes up and down over time by about 4 to 5 lbs (2 kg) or more. If your weight goes up 5 lb one day, it does not follow that it will continue to do this.

Rapid weight changes are not normal but do occur as part of bulimia nervosa due to fluid shifts (chapter 5). It is therefore pointless to try to check and control your body by weighing yourself daily.

- Be bold: give your scales away, or put them in an place where you can't reach them easily (the loft or the cellar).
- Or, if you aren't quite brave enough to do that, draw up a timetable with plans for a gradual reduction in the number of times you weigh yourself.

### Is Weight the Only Important Indicator of Health?

No. Recent research shows that the ratio of your waist measurement to your hip measurement is a better predictor of health than is weight. Your waist size divided by your hip size should be less than 0.9, i.e. your waist should be less than nine-tenths of your hip size. The traditional pear shape of women, although currently devalued, is a shape associated with health and a low risk of illness.

### Cavemen Didn't Eat Ice-cream

Evolution and our genes have not yet caught up with two new things in our environment to which we now have to adapt: (1) Most of us have little or no exercise. (2) Our diet contains a high degree of fat, with high-fat items being promoted as special, luxurious, romantic, or even sexy (think of those ice-cream ads). In other words, it is much easier to get fat while leading a modern Western life style than if you were Neanderthal man.

### Diets Don't Work

The greatest pressure to lose weight is on those members of our society who have a tendency to being overweight as part of their constitution. One conclusion drawn at a recent conference on obesity by the eminent scientist, Dr Kalucy, was that DIETS DO NOT WORK. He instructs all his obese patients to stop dieting, and they subsequently lose weight. Can this be true? All diets used to treat obesity can produce a 5% weight loss in the short term, but after a year the weight increases again to its normal, higher value.

- Go to your local bookshop, and see how many books and magazines there are on slimming and diets. How can there be such a big market for these items? Why are new diets and diet books published each year? The answer is, of course, that they do not work. Slimming is marketed as any other hobby, something that will entrap you for life.

Even doctors are affected by the propaganda, and they may suggest to you that a lower weight may be healthy for you.

*Georgina*
Georgina went to her general practitioner with a problem with her feet. He weighed her and said that she was overweight. She began to diet and lost weight, but soon she developed bulimia. Twenty years later she presented to a specialised clinic; her teeth were destroyed,  and surgeons were advising her to have her large intestine removed to remedy her chronic constipation and stomach pain as a result of chronic abuse of laxatives.

## THE HEALTH HAZARDS OF DIETING

Recent evidence from a large study in America, reported in *The New England Journal of Medicine*, shows that people whose weight has fluctuated often or greatly—i.e. who have gone on many diets—have a higher risk of dying from heart disease. The conclusion from this study was that the risk of early death was as high in those who went on many diets as in those who were massively obese. This was particularly important in the youngest group of patients.

### Dieting is Dangerous
Weight loss has profound effects on your physical and psychological health.

*The Effects of Starvation on the Body*
1. Sensitivity to cold: this includes cold extremities, which may lead to chilblains.
2. Sleep disturbances: waking up early or several times in the night.
3. Weak bladder: passing water frequently throughout the day or night.
4. Excess hair growth on the body.
5. Poor circulation, slow pulse, and fainting spells.
6. Thin bones: with time this may result in fractures, leading to pain and deformity.

7. Periods stop or become very irregular. It is usually only possible for a woman to have periods when 15% of her body is composed of fat.
8. The stomach shrinks and feels uncomfortably distended after eating even a small amount of food.
9. Gut function is decreased, and constipation results.
10. The bone marrow, where the red and white cells in the blood are formed, is sluggish, which can result in anaemia.
11. The lack of nourishment to the liver damages it so that it is unable to manufacture body proteins. This may result in swelling of the ankles and legs.
12. The blood cholesterol level is increased. This results from the lack of oestrogen (women before their menopause are protected from heart attacks by oestrogen) and because of abnormal liver function.
13. General tiredness may lead to muscular weakness and paralysis.
14. In young girls, growth may be stunted and puberty delayed.

*The Effects of Starvation upon the Mind*
1. Mood is lowered, with tearfulness and pessimism.
2. The mind becomes preoccupied with food, and there is often a strong urge to overeat.
3. The ability and interest in forming relationships is diminished.
4. Concentration is poor, and it is difficult to function fully.
5. Minor problems appear insurmountable.
6. Complex thought is impaired.

These lists are very dry and dull, but many authors have written about the effects of starvation. We suggest you read *One Day in the Life of Ivan Denisovich* by Alexander Solzhenitsyn, Kurt Vonnegut's *Slaughterhouse-five*, and *Castaway* by R. Irwin, to see how starvation affects human thinking and behaviour.

You may say: I did lose weight when my problem started, but since then I have put on weight. So can the problems above still apply to me? The answer is yes, definitely, as a common pattern is to alternate fasting with bingeing. If you don't eat for over four hours, your body will start to go into starvation mode and switch all the metabolic processes to those that conserve energy.

## HOW MUCH DO I NEED TO EAT?
Appetite is tightly linked to energy expenditure. This is known as metabolic rate. Your body has to work harder and will need more energy when you exercise or if you are in a cold climate. Hormonal changes in our body also affect metabolism. Women in the second half of their menstrual cycles are metabolically more active as their bodies prepare

themselves for egg implantation. One sign of this increased metabolism is the increase in body temperature seen after ovulation. You may have been aware of your increased appetite premenstrually and are frightened by it.

You can see from the above that there are no easy rules. People differ in the amount of energy they need, and all the factors mentioned above alter your energy requirements. As soon as you cut down your food intake, your body will clamp down on its energy expenditure, and losing weight will be more difficult. Your body will do this more quickly and more efficiently the more times you try to diet. This has been called weight cycling and has led a wit to describe it as the "rhythm method of girth control".

You should need to eat at least between 1,500 and 2,000 calories per day. However, if your levels of activity are high or you are still growing, you may need considerably more. However, we suggest that you do not try to count calories but judge portion sizes from those that other people eat or those available to be bought.

## WORKING WITH YOUR BODY TO OBTAIN YOUR OPTIMAL WEIGHT AND SHAPE

Long gaps between meals switch the body into storage mode, and so nutrients will be selectively deposited in storage depots on the expectation of famine. The balance between fat and lean body tissue is disturbed, and so weight may increase to keep the amount of lean tissue constant. Eating only at night does the same sort of thing. At this time the body's hormones prepare for the fast during sleep and promote storage of energy into fat deposits.

*Imelda*

Imelda came to London from Northern Ireland to marry her boyfriend. She quickly had a baby and found it difficult to keep contact with her old work colleagues. Her husband's friends were not very welcoming towards her, and she felt very isolated. With her family in Northern Ireland, she had nobody she could turn to for help. Her eating became chaotic. Each morning she would wake up and vow to eat nothing, and, indeed, she would eat no meals. However, when she came home after finishing her shopping, having eaten nothing all day, the prospect of her son turning the sitting room to chaos led her to eat 6 to 7 bags of crisps, followed by a chocolate bar. To make up for this, she would redouble her efforts to avoid meals the next day. All the time her weight increased steadily.

To work with your body, you need to:

- Eat the majority of your food before evening.
- Eat small amounts regularly throughout the day.
- Exercise regularly, though not excessively.
- Restrict your consumption of fat but ensure that protein and carbohydrate are adequate.
- Avoid multiple courses.

## Making a Start

The first step to get your eating under control is to ensure that you are eating regularly throughout the day. You may say, "If I start eating in the morning, I will binge all day." Yes, you are right, there may be a brief phase when you will be unable to stop eating after a meal, and you will have to take extra precautions, but the goal of regular meals throughout the day is essential.

You must not try to lose weight at this stage. If you do, the vicious circles of bulimia will just go on and on. You may say, "I can't give up trying to lose weight. It is too important." Yes, it is very tough to let go of something that is very important to you. Perhaps it is easiest if you just persuade yourself to put losing weight on hold for a while (a day, a week, a month, 6 months at a time). That way, it will be less frightening.

Also, once your eating is less chaotic, your weight may decrease, or the balance between fat and lean tissue may get more acceptable.

*Plan A: For Those without Any Pattern to Their Eating*
- If your eating pattern is totally chaotic, set a goal of re-introducing regular meals one by one. For example, could you manage a baked potato with cottage cheese for lunch? Do not be too ambitious, but do be honest with yourself. Choose something you feel safe in eating, preferably with safeguards to end the meal. Can you promise to eat this item every day? Expect it to be two steps forward and one back. Keep persisting. Every normal meal you eat is a small victory.
- Draw up a list of ten small meals that you think would be easiest for you to attempt to eat.
- Rank them in order of difficulty, with the most difficult at the bottom.
- Start with the meal at the top of the list.
- Plan to eat that meal at some time in the day before 3 p.m.

How can you ensure that this will not lead to a binge?
Ask yourself:

- Could I eat the meal with someone else?
- Could I eat this meal in a canteen or cafe?

- Could I have something I enjoy doing timetabled for half an hour after my meal?

YOUR ANXIETY AND GUILT LEVELS BEFORE, DURING AND AFTER THIS MEAL WILL BE HIGH. To deal with anxiety and guilt:

- Take a piece of paper or booklet and a pencil.
- Draw a vertical line and mark it 0–10 (0 = no anxiety; 10 = utter panic or overwhelming guilt)
- Put a mark where your anxiety/guilt level is now.
- Every 5 minutes, mark off what your level of anxiety/guilt is whilst eating and for 2 hours after eating.
- What exactly are the thoughts going through your mind now that are leading to these emotions? These thoughts may be vague and jumbled—that doesn't matter. Jot them down, even if they seem incomplete, frightening, or silly.
- Try to keep adding to the list over the next few hours.
- The next day, when you repeat your meal, take out your book and repeat this process—and so on, every day.
- Later, when you are relaxed, take out your booklet and paper, and re-read these thoughts that you have written.
- Either show them to a close friend, or imagine showing them to a close friend.
- What would they say about your thoughts about food?
- Get them to read this chapter. What would they say now about your thoughts?
- Write down exactly what they would say in your book.
- At the end of their replies to each of your list of thoughts about eating, indicate on a scale of 0 to 10 how much you agree with what they have said.
- Repeat this process each day.
- Try to catch any new thoughts you may have when faced with food.
- Try to make up your own replies to these ideas.
- Keep eating exactly the same meal each day with the same routine until your anxiety level at the beginning of the meal has fallen by at least 2 points. Then you may be ready to try to eat the next item on your list.
- With the next meal, go through exactly the same procedure as before. Once you have been able to tackle two different meals, try to eat two meals before 3 p.m. each day. Go through exactly the same procedure as before. The next stage, thereafter, will be to have two meals and a snack before 3 p.m. each day. Do not worry if your diet is rather monotonous at the moment.

*Plan B: For Those with Some Degree of Order to Their Eating*
If your eating pattern is reasonably regular, what is the size of your meal? Are you eating sufficient calories early in the day?

- Gradually plan to shift your eating so that more calories are eaten earlier in the day. You should aim to eat 30% at breakfast and 40% for lunch.

## HOW TO RELEARN EATING CONTROL

- Try to eat in a room that is separate from where food is stored and prepared. Eat all your meals in this place.
- Make every meal look as appetizing and attractive as possible.
- Lay out a table-cloth or place-mat and serviette.
- Make your place setting as attractive as possible.
- Bring your plate in from a different room, leaving behind all the food containers in the other room.
- Don't distract yourself with television, radio, or reading. This 15 minutes is set aside to relearn about food.
- Spend 30 seconds looking at your plate before you begin. Put down your knife and fork between each mouthful. What does the plate look like now? Make sure you know how the food tastes and feels in your mouth. Take longer before you swallow.

### What Should I Eat and When?

The ideal target is three meals almost equally divided calorifically and each well balanced for protein (e.g. cheese, eggs, meat, fish, beans) and carbohydrate (e.g. bread, pasta, potatoes, rice), with small snacks in-between.

Remember these tips:

- Protein is more satisfying, calorie-for-calorie, than other food items.
- Hot food is more satisfying than cold food.
- Solid food is more satisfying than liquid food.

Ensure that there is no gap longer than 3 hours without a small snack, e.g. coffee and some fruit.

Table 3.1 shows the diet plan of Thelma, who had gained weight with bulimia. She was pleasantly surprised that she lost weight following this plan.

TABLE 3.1
Thelma's Diet Plan

| Time | Meal | What eaten |
|------|------|-----------|
| 8.15 | Breakfast | Fruit juice, 1 individual box of cereal, 200 ml skimmed milk, 1 slice of brown bread, 1 pat margarine, 1 spoon marmalade, 1 pot of tea or coffee |
| 10.30 | Mid-morning snack | Coffee with milk (skimmed), 1 piece of fruit |
| 12.30 | Lunch | Main course: piece of grilled meat with rice and salad or vegetarian dish<br>Pudding: yoghurt, fruit salad or fruit, 1 cup of tea/coffee |
| 3.30 | Mid-afternoon snack | Tea with skimmed milk, piece of fruit or yoghurt or 2 plain savoury biscuits |
| 6.30 | Supper | Main course: same as lunch—fruit/yoghurt, 1 cup of water, 1 cup of tea with skimmed milk |
|  | Bedtime | Hot drink with skimmed milk |

- It may be easier if you follow exactly the same diet each day and gradually make exchanges so that the variety of your food is gradually increased, e.g. fish rather than chicken, or a pear for a snack rather than an apple.
- Take it slowly. It is difficult to change long-standing habits.

## How Can I Judge What Amount to Eat?

You are right to think that this is difficult.

- Eat with other people, and have portions the same size as theirs.
- Buy individual meals (frozen or long-life).
- Avoid artificial sweeteners. These feed misinformation into your body. Your body is tricked by the artificial sweetener, and years of learning about the metabolic consequences of food is undone. Your body will learn: sweetness = no or little energy. Your body's instincts will therefore drive you to eat large quantities of sweet things as it strives for adequate nourishment.

## How to End your Meals

There are many signals that the body uses to finish eating. All of these get upset with bulimia nervosa.

1. How a meal looks: all living creatures learn to predict how much energy and nutrients they will later absorb from a given food just by the look of it.

2. The taste and smell of foods are clues that remind our body what effect a given food will have on our blood sugar.
3. The feeling of fullness in our stomach is another sign to indicate that we have had sufficient nutrition.
4. Finally, hunger is satisfied for several hours by the nutrients that are absorbed into the blood.

As these normal ways of ending meals have been disturbed with bulimia nervosa, you may initially need to make triggers to end a meal.

*Susan*

Susan knew that whenever, and whatever, she ate, she would end up bingeing. She also could eat nothing with others, though she was able to confide in others and ask them to help. She asked her friend to knock on her door 15 minutes after starting a meal, go with her to put her food away, take her locker key, and sit and have coffee with her for an hour.

Alternatively, you could use food substances to signal the end of a meal.

*Katie*

Katie lived alone in a flat, and she devised a plan of eating a plain grapefruit at the end of each meal. The ritual of peeling, and then the sharp, bitter taste, was a powerful ending signal.

There are many other ways that you will be able to think of and use successfully. Spend some time thinking of alternative triggers, which you could use to end your meals.

CHAPTER FOUR

# Bingeing, Nibbling, and Compulsive Overeating: The Black Hole of the Never-satisfied Stomach

The term "bulimia" means "eating like an ox". Most people with a bulimic disorder see binges as the central and most unpleasant aspect of their eating difficulties.

*Andrew*

Andrew, a 22-year-old student, described his binges as follows: "Once I've started, I stuff myself till I am completely full and bloated. I worry sometimes that my stomach might burst. I can hardly breathe. I eat very quickly, and I barely notice what I put into my mouth. I don't chew the food. The worst thing about it is this feeling of being totally out of control, of having to go on eating, it takes me over. I cannot stop until I'm absolutely stuffed."

People vary greatly in the kinds of food they eat during a binge and in the amount consumed. We define a binge as any large amount of food that is eaten rapidly in an out-of-control fashion. Mild bouts of overeating are part of many people's lives and are not unhealthy.

Other people don't exactly binge, but instead they follow a somewhat different pattern of overeating—so-called grazing or compulsive overeating, i.e. someone who nibbles all day without being able to stop.

*Sonya*

Sonya had a very difficult childhood, with her parents getting divorced when she was six. Thereafter her mother had a seemingly endless stream of boyfriends. "When a new man was on the scene, my mother hardly noticed my existence. They'd be out together most nights of the week. She'd give me lots of pocket-money though, to keep me quiet. After a while, things would go wrong, and there would be arguments, sometimes physical fights. Then the boyfriend would get kicked out, and I would be left with a mother who was miserable and bad-tempered, who withdrew to her bedroom for days. I had nothing to turn to apart from food. I remember sitting there day in, day out, eating one biscuit or sweet after another, to make that horrible loneliness go away. By the age of 13 I weighed 12 stone, although I am only 5 ft tall. At school nobody wanted to be my friend. So I ate more."

Even though Sonya now is in a stable relationship with a supportive partner, when he isn't around, she overeats. "My partner often has to go on business trips, he may be away for a few days at a time. When I am alone in the house I just eat all day, slowly and steadily. It is as if I constantly have to keep my hands and mouth busy. Sometimes I think it is to do with getting flashbacks of this old feeling of having nobody who cares. At other times I haven't got a clue why I do it, I just nibble all day".

In what follows below, we focus our discussion mainly on bingeing; however, if you graze, nibble, comfort-eat, or compulsively overeat, the descriptions below of the mechanisms involved will also apply to you.

Most people binge/graze/comfort-eat on high-calorie foods, which may be sweet or savory. Some people overeat on food that they secretly love but see as "unhealthy" or "forbidden" and therefore only eat during a binge. Others eat whatever comes their way, even food they don't like. Some people go as far as eating frozen food or scavenging through rubbish bins to find something to eat. The experience of overeating regularly is highly demoralising and makes most people feel that they have failed abysmally.

## WHY IS MY EATING UNCONTROLLED?

Bingeing is not the result of being a weak-willed person. There are a number of important physiological and psychological reasons for bingeing.

### Physiological Reasons

Bingeing can be the direct result of starvation. By giving you strong cravings for food, your body will tell you loud and clear that it is not getting enough nutrition. These cravings can be constant or intermittent. The harder you try to cut your food intake down, the more you will be prone to bingeing. Often people make things worse by cutting out meals after a binge to make up for having eaten so much. This will automatically programme the next binge. Alcohol and drugs, which reduce inhibitions, may also make you binge more.

### Psychological Reasons

Boredom, depression, stress, tension, and loneliness often lead to bingeing, as food, at least at the start of a binge, is comforting and eases these negative feelings. Sometimes a small slip from a rigid and inadequate diet may make you so demoralised that you decide to give up control completely and have a binge.

Physiological and psychological reasons for bingeing are not mutually exclusive and often occur in the same person at the same time.

## HOW TO STOP BINGES

A lot of people feel that if only their binges could be cured, they wouldn't have a problem. Unfortunately bingeing as a symptom can't be treated in isolation. In trying to tackle the physiological aspects of bingeing, it is very important:

- that you work on eating regularly at meal-times (see chapter 2) to give your body proper nutrition and thereby to reduce strong cravings for food that are going to set you off again;
- to try as hard as you can not to omit meals after bingeing, as this will programme the next binge.
- that you deal with the consequences of bingeing, e.g. vomiting (see chapter 5).

If you treat these aspects of your problem, you will soon find that binges decrease in duration and frequency.

### Am I Addicted to Sugar?

Many people without an eating disorder have a sweet tooth. However, for sufferers of bulimia, cravings for sweet things can be so powerful that it feels like an addiction to sugar. You may also have the experience that, once you have had some sweets, you need to have more and more and more, reinforcing your sense of total powerlessness *vis-à-vis* sweets. Sugary foods are taken into our bloodstream more quickly than other foods. This increase in blood sugar leads to the hormone, insulin, being released, which facilitates the uptake of sugar into body cells, with the result that the blood sugar is lowered. Low blood sugar leads to the desire to eat more sweet things. This effect is particularly marked if you are undernourished. Also, if you drink large amounts of artificially sweetened diet drinks, your body will have learnt to associate the pleasant taste of sweetness with little nutritional value and will drive you to eat large amounts.

Some sweet foods, like chocolaty things, lead to the release of endorphines, morphine-like "happy-making" substances produced by the brain, making it very rewarding to eat this type of sweet.

However, you will find that if you follow the advice given in chapter 3 and work on eating more normally, the feeling of being addicted to sweets will lessen and even disappear completely, so there is no need to give up sweets altogether. As long as your eating pattern is very chaotic, it is probably wise to be careful with sweets and only to eat them in conjunction with some other food (to avoid getting low blood sugar after eating the sweet). Once you have a bit more control over your eating, to have a small amount of chocolate or cake every day may be a task to set yourself, to prove to yourself that you can tackle danger foods.

## Dealing with the Psychological Aspects of Bingeing

You need to get to know your own triggers, which will be influenced by your body and mind. Your diary will help with this (see chapter 1). Here are some examples from former sufferers:

### Anna

Anna, a 23-year-old woman, had a long journey to work, during which she had to change buses several times. "Each time I got off the bus, I walked past one or two sweet shops and I'd buy myself something else." Because Anna knew that she would binge on her journey to work, she never allowed herself any breakfast.

Anna decided to have a regular breakfast before going out. She also realised that she got extremely bored on her long bus journey (she couldn't read on the bus as this made her feel sick). Her solution to this was to find an alternative route, which meant she could take the train and read. These simple measures improved her bingeing greatly.

### Belinda

Belinda started work at lunch-time. Mornings were a boring, unstructured time for her. There was nobody to have breakfast with as she liked to get up late and her mother was up very early. Sometimes Belinda would exercise in the morning, which she didn't enjoy but felt was good for her. However, when she was tired after a late night, she could not motivate herself to do her exercise, and she would have a binge instead. Belinda's solution was to do something she liked before work that would get her out of the house. She arranged to attend acting lessons in the morning, and her bingeing improved.

*Ros*

When Ros came to our clinic, she binged four to six times a week. Binges could happen at any time during the day, in different places. There did not seem to be any particular pattern. She felt very out of control and couldn't say what triggered her binges. She was asked to put into her diary a minute account of everything that happened from the moment she first had the thought of bingeing to the moment when she actually binged. It became clear that very often before an actual binge there would be a build-up of several hours during which small things would go wrong. This would lead to increasing frustration and would often result in a binge. On one day, for example, she was bored at work. At 2.00 p.m. she thought of bingeing for the first time. She rejected the thought firmly and distracted herself with a computer game. By 4.00 p.m. she was bored again, and the thought of bingeing came back. A friend then rang and cancelled their evening outing. At that point she went to the bank and drew some money out to buy food for her binge. She then made an attempt to contact another friend to go out but was turned down. By that point she was so upset that she went home and binged.

Over a period of time Ros became very good at identifying "danger" situations. She realised that she had used bingeing as an easy solution to many minor irritations in her life. For each "danger" situation she learnt to find a more appropriate way of dealing with it. For example, boredom at work was a recurring problem (she was a receptionist, and there were long stretches of sitting about without doing anything). She decided to do some reading towards a part-time degree course whilst at work, so that she didn't feel she had wasted the whole day. She decided that if friends let her down for evening arrangements, she would go to the cinema on her own instead, rather than sit at home and mope which would invariably lead to a binge.

The example of Karen, shows that even if you understand the psychological reasons for your binges, it may not always be easy to give them up very quickly, especially if there is a strong element of comfort.

*Karen*

Karen was a single working mother in her thirties. She had been sexually abused as a child. When she first came to see us, she binged and vomited several times a day. She then learnt to eat more during the day and only binged and vomited once at night, which she was very pleased about. She kept saying she wanted to improve more and give up bingeing and vomiting altogether, but somehow she couldn't. After a lot of discussion about why she had got so stuck at this point, it turned out that she felt her life was a constant struggle. She greatly missed having a partner who cared for her, but at the same time she was extremely frightened of entering a relationship with a man, given her traumatic childhood experience. She identified that bingeing was the only thing in her life that was easy, pleasurable, and comforting and made her lonely evenings more bearable.

These examples show that there are many different patterns of bingeing. You may need to monitor yourself using your diary for one to two weeks to get to know your own pattern.

- Once you have got to know your pattern a bit better, try to "play around" with it a little to increase your sense of control. Try to limit your binges to just one place. Alternatively try to restrict your bingeing to just part of the day.
- Write down a list of situations that trigger your binges and find ways of dealing with them.
- Try to anticipate danger-zones. Weekends with a lot of unstructured time are prime bingeing time for many. Draw up a time-table of pleasurable activities for the week end, and stick to it.
- Whenever you feel like bingeing, distract yourself by doing something that is incompatible with bingeing, like going for a walk, phoning or seeing a friend. Watching television and reading are not very helpful in this respect, as it is very easy to binge whilst you are watching. Many of the adverts are designed to promote dissatisfaction with ourselves as we are or encourage us to consume more.
- Don't do your food shopping when you are hungry.
- Don't get your parents/partner/flat-mate to lock the kitchen door. This is bound to make you want the food inside even more, and you will almost certainly find a way in.
- Don't blame yourself if you have had a binge. Look carefully at the behaviour chain, and spot the links that you could have broken. Work through in your mind what would have happened if you had made a shift. You will have learned something for next time (go to chapter 8, which discusses slips).
- A lot of people get very frightened if they haven't binged for a while. They feel that any binge would send them back to "square one". To prove to yourself that this is not the case, it is often useful to have a

planned binge. Remember, a small setback can't undo the good work you have done for weeks.
- Try to avoid people, places, and things that are associated with bingeing for you.
- Get in touch with someone you know who has had bulimia and has been able to control it. Find out what worked for them.

## Coping with Cravings and Urges

- Monitor your urges to eat, and rate their severity (on a 1–10 scale) and duration.
- Make a note of what effect your expected eating would have on your thoughts, feelings, and physical state, as discussed in the example of Cherry below.

*Cherry*
  Cherry noticed that her urges to binge occurred when she was lonely. She had not gone out with the rest of the family but had stayed at home to study. She wrote in her diary that she expected that a binge would get rid of her loneliness and her anger about having to work.

When you review your diary by yourself or with your support, try to draw up a list of the activities that would produce the effect that you sought when you binged. Some of your urges to eat will be started by the normal drives of appetite in response to hunger. Others are started by external factors. Urges are an entirely normal reaction, and you will need to develop several different strategies to deal with them.

- *Detachment:* Do not identify with the urge. Instead of thinking "I'm dying to binge", change your thoughts to "I'm experiencing an urge to overeat—it will get strong but then it will go". Allow yourself to experience the urge, "let it be". You don't have to give in to it. You may believe that if you don't give in to the urge, you will go mad or some other catastrophe will occur—it won't. If you do not give in to the urge, it will eventually weaken and go away.
- *Imagery:* Imagine that the urge to eat is like a wave. Let yourself surf along the top of the urge without losing your balance. Don't let the force of it suck you under.
    Imagine the urge as an ALIEN MONSTER. As soon as you recognise its presence, dispose of it quickly by chopping off its head.
    Imagine the urge as a growth inside you. You are a surgeon with a scalpel who can cut it out.
- *Logic:* Whenever you start to think of the positive short term benefits of eating, counteract these thoughts by thinking about the long term negative consequences.

- *Distraction:* Make a list of alternative activities you can do to take your mind off the urge.

If your trigger is anger or frustration, other ways of coping may be more helpful. An assertive response may be needed (see chapter 11).

## LAPSES

Lapses will occur—they are a definite and important part of recovery. Simply regard them as challenges or learning experiences. The most important thing is to take them in your stride and not think that you are back to square one.

### What to Do if You Do Lapse

- Stop and think! Try to intervene as soon as possible, and extract yourself from the situation.
- Keep calm! Observe yourself with detachment. Your first reaction will be to feel guilty and blame yourself—let these feelings slowly ebb away. Remember, this is a normal part of recovery.
- Renew your commitment: Get out your balance sheet and letters, and study them again. Think of how far you have come. Remake your decision. You can be in control.
- Review the situation that led to the lapse. Were there early warning signals? Did you make an attempt to cope? What have your learnt for next time.
- Take charge: Put into play one of your coping techniques—and leave the house.
- Get help: Now is the time that your supporter can be of greatest value. Get in touch with your co-therapist immediately.

# CHAPTER FIVE

# Vomiting, Laxatives, and Diuretics : Have Your Cake and Eat It—Or Not?

You may have read, heard about, or even discovered for yourself other methods of controlling your weight apart from restricting intake. The commonest methods chosen are making yourself vomit or taking laxatives or diuretics. Often these methods of "weight-control" are started when a person feels that dieting alone doesn't have the desired effect, or once binges have begun. Part of you may feel, "I can have my cake and eat it"— however, this is far from the truth. Part of you is probably somewhat ashamed and worried about using these practices. You are right to be worried.

## FACING THE FACTS

Let's go through the facts first. How good are these methods at controlling weight? Although vomiting may get rid of 30 to 50% of calories eaten, depending on how soon after eating you do it and on how long you have used vomiting as a regular practice, it never leads to sustained weight loss. The more you vomit, the more your body will crave food. This will result in more bingeing, which then makes you want to vomit more. A vicious circle has started ...

Laxatives and diuretics do not lead to any loss of calories. Yes, you are right, they may reduce weight, but this is only temporary, and it is due to loss of body fluid. Your body protects against loss of water by producing a variety of hormones called anti-diuretic hormone, aldosterone, and renin, which are released generously in response to any loss of fluid. These hormones then lead to water retention, which will make you feel bloated and heavy. You may even notice swelling around your eyes in the morning, in your belly, and, at the end of the day, in your ankles. This will make you want to step up the dose of the laxatives or diuretics you are taking. Another vicious circle ...

Taking laxatives regularly over a period of time makes your guts lazy and will give you constipation. Gradually you will have to increase the amount of laxatives you are taking. The more you take, the more constipated you will become. You have entered yet another vicious circle ...

## WHY YOU ARE RIGHT TO WORRY

A number of health problems are commonly caused by these practices. You need to know about these:

- Vomiting, laxatives and diuretics lead to a loss of blood salts and water. This commonly produces CHRONIC TIREDNESS, WEAKNESS, INABILITY TO CONCENTRATE, DIZZINESS, HEADACHES and PALPITATIONS. You also need to know that EPILEPTIC FITS, IRREGULAR HEARTBEAT and KIDNEY DAMAGE may be caused by these practices.
- Stomach acid brought up by vomiting dissolves the enamel of your teeth. This makes teeth sensitive and vulnerable to cavities.
- Your salivary glands around your mouth may swell up because they are working overtime to produce more saliva when you vomit. Although this is not dangerous, it can be painful at times. It will make your face look fat and bloated. You may even look as if you have mumps. This may make you think you ought to lose more weight and may make you vomit more. Another vicious circle ...!
- Vomiting may damage your gullet. Stomach pain and vomiting blood are common. Regurgitation of food may become habitual.
- Chronic laxative use may destroy the small nerves in your gut, which may lead to gut paralysis. This is a potentially life-threatening complication, requiring surgical treatment. Your back passage may start to come down when you strain on the toilet.
- Circle which of these health problems apply to you:

| | |
|---|---|
| Chronic tiredness | Vomiting blood |
| Hair loss | Dental problems |
| Weakness | Fits |
| Inability to concentrate | Irregular heartbeat |
| Dizziness | Constipation |
| Headaches | Bleeding from your bottom |
| Palpitations | Something coming down, down below |
| Stomach pain | Kidney stones |

Bloating                          Kidney infection
Kidney failure                    Ankle swelling
Irregular periods

Most of these problems are reversible and will improve quickly if vomiting and the use of laxatives and diuretics are stopped. If none of these medical problems apply to you at the moment, you may feel somewhat reassured. You should bear in mind that some of them take time to develop.

## WHAT TYPE OF WEIGHT CONTROLLER ARE YOU?

People vary enormously in their attitudes to vomiting, laxatives, and diuretics.

*Type A:* Some people see it as a kind of physical necessity to make themselves sick. They do not see themselves as responsible or playing an active part in it. Take Carla, a 25-year-old actress, whose eating disorder had started when she was 15. "When I've binged I feel terribly full. I feel physically sick. It's agony. I don't actually make myself sick. I just bend over and the food comes out. It just happens."

*Type B:* Other people see vomiting/laxatives/diuretics as a kind of habit, a part of their daily routine.
*Natasha:* "Vomiting is just like brushing my teeth. I don't feel much when I do it. It makes me feel clean. I couldn't do without it."
*Lily:* "I always take five laxative tablets after every meal. I have got so used to it. I hardly think about it."

*Type C:* Yet other people find these practices very painful and humiliating.
*Susan:* "I hate sticking my head down the loo every day. I am so ashamed of myself. How did I get into this? How could I sink so low? Afterwards I feel totally devastated and tell myself it will never happen again. But then it does and all the agony starts again."
*Sheila:* "Yesterday I had a 5-hour binge. I panicked totally and took 80 laxative tablets. I spent the whole night on the loo. I was in such a lot of pain. I felt disgusted with myself and yet I couldn't help feeling I had somehow deserved it."

Circle which of these types describes your own response most accurately:

Type A   Type B   Type C   Other (describe):

If you feel type A or B describes what you feel about your vomiting, laxative or diuretic abuse, you should ask yourself whether it has always been like this. You have allowed yourself to become cut-off from the pain of it. You do need to try to get in touch with these feelings again. The more cut-off you are from the negative aspects (pain, danger, shame) of your vomiting or laxative/diuretic abuse, the more difficult it will be to stop.

## HOW TO STOP VOMITING

Follow Plan A if you:

- only make yourself sick 2 to 3 times per week; or
- often induce vomiting several hours after bingeing; or
- sometimes don't vomit at all after bingeing.

Follow Plan B if you:

- vomit most days; or
- vomit after snacks, meals, and binges.

*Plan A:* You have quite a bit of control over your vomiting, even though it may not appear so to you. The following plan is designed to give you even more control.

- Look back over the last 2–3 weeks. What has been the maximum number of times you have been sick per week?
- Over the next week try to be sick once less often than the maximum number of times per week you were sick before.
- If you manage to do this easily, cut down the number of times of vomiting you "allow" yourself by one further episode the week after.
- If you can only do this with difficulty, repeat the same step until it becomes easier.
- Continue like this, cutting down every week or every other week, until you have stopped vomiting.

A bit of general advice before you start: always write your goal for the week into your diary at the beginning of the week and then try to stick to it. Try to stick to your goal exactly. But don't aim to change too quickly.

- If you have had an extra binge, try, if at all possible, to keep the food inside you. If that is too difficult, try at least to delay the vomiting. This will make you very anxious. Use the coping techniques described under Plan B.
- If you were sick more often than you had decided to be one week, go back to last week's goal. (Remember, getting better often involves taking two steps forward and one step back.) Maybe you were a bit too ambitious last week!

*Plan B:* You have become very used to making yourself sick as a way of dealing with anxieties about gaining weight and perhaps other anxieties too. To un-learn this will be difficult. At present you probably only know two modes of existing—either being painfully full or being completely empty. Most people without an eating disorder know many states in-between, which range from being slightly hungry to being pleasantly full after a meal. You need to get used to the "in-between states" again. This is best achieved by a step-wise delay of vomiting.

- Think back over the last week or two. On average, what is your time-gap between eating and being sick?
- Over the next week, try to delay being sick regularly for this length of time.
- The week after, increase the time gap a little, and so on. Move to a new, longer time-interval when you reliably achieve this week's goal.
- If you always vomit straight after eating, you may want to start with delaying vomiting for a very short time only, say 5 minutes each time. It is better to go for a modest target and achieve this reliably than to be too ambitious.

## How to Cope with Your Anxiety

Delaying vomiting will make you very anxious. You will probably feel terribly bloated, and your fears about gaining weight will rise sky-high.

- The best technique for coping with anxiety is to try to distract yourself by, for example, ringing a friend, being with other people, going for a walk, or by using the techniques of detachment and imagery described in chapter 4. Going to the bottle bank and smashing a few bottles can be good fun and helps release tension. (Watching television or reading are usually less successful as there is always a loo nearby!)

### Margaret

Margaret, a 35-year-old housewife and mother of two children, enjoyed needlework, and so she decided to use sewing as a distraction technique. Every time she felt like being sick, she knitted an extra square for a patchwork blanket. "Knitting helped me to keep my anxieties down. At the same time, to see the patchwork blanket grow made me feel that I had channelled my anxieties into something useful."

### Judith

Judith, on the other hand, found a spiritual solution for herself. "Normally I would say the rosary when I wanted to be sick, but if the anxieties got very strong I went to my local church and prayed."

- It is important that you find something that might work for you!
- Some people find it useful to write down some reassuring or frightening statements on a card that they carry around with them. Some even compose a comic song or jingle in which they make a joke of themselves.

### Elizabeth

Elizabeth was a very gifted singer. On hearing that vomiting might make her hoarse, she decided to write on a card, "I want to be a singer. I don't want to damage my voice. I don't have to rely on vomiting." Every time she wanted to be sick, she pulled out her card and read the statements out loud to herself. "To read the statements on the card aloud gave me more strength to resist."

### Susan

Susan, who often took up to 100 laxative tablets in one go, wrote a card to herself, saying, "If I carry on like this I will damage my health severely. I must stop". She got this card out a few times when she felt the urge to take laxatives, but she soon gave up, as thinking about the health consequences of her laxative abuse just increased her sense of panic.

In writing a card, you can see from the example of Susan that it is often better to write down something that is specific to you (not a general statement) and also something positive, rather than focusing on the negative.

### Golden Rules

- Try one thing at a time, for a week at a time.
- If you fail, make things easier and try again.
- Especially if you follow Plan B, it is very important that you find ways of rewarding yourself if you achieve your weekly target, as otherwise, with each weekly step being small, it may be difficult to remember that you are doing well. Here is a list of possible rewards from which you may want to choose. Think of ideas which you might add to the list. Buy yourself something nice:

  a book
  a bunch of flowers
  a plant
  some earrings
  a day in the country

- Until you have managed to give up vomiting completely, you need to know that YOU SHOULD NOT BRUSH YOUR TEETH IMMEDIATELY AFTER VOMITING, as it rubs in the acid and makes things worse. It is better simply to rinse your mouth either with water or with a bicarbonate or fluoride solution.

## HOW TO STOP ABUSING LAXATIVES, DIURETICS, AND OTHER MEDICATIONS

Especially if you have been taking laxatives or diuretics on a daily basis in fairly large amounts, you may find that if you stop them suddenly, this will lead to "rebound" fluid retention, which can cause gross swelling. It may be easier to cut down your laxatives/diuretics gradually. You can do this either by cutting down on the number of laxatives you take each day or by gradually increasing the number of laxative/diuretic-free days per week.

### Coping with Constipation

Giving up laxatives will invariably make you constipated for a while. This is bound to make you feel uncomfortable and bloated. Remember, many women are prone to constipation anyway and do not have a regular daily bowel movement.

- Including fruit and vegetables in your diet will help.
- A hot drink before eating in the morning stimulates the bowels.
- Do not eat too much bran, as this will result in stomach distention and flatulence.
- Replace laxatives on a one-to-one basis with prunes or other dried fruit.

### Coping with Swelling (Oedema)

Despite cutting down your laxatives/diuretics gradually, you may still, for a while, be prone to developing oedema. To prevent this:

- Consider sleeping propped up, to avoid oedema collecting around the face.
- Try to sit with legs up to help the oedema drain from your ankles.

# CHAPTER SIX

# Learning to Feel Good about Your Body

Many people with bulimia feel extremely bad about their body. They treat it, not as a part of themselves, but as a hated enemy that they would like to get rid of. They constantly watch it, criticise it, and struggle against it. Many sufferers of bulimia can't face looking at themselves naked, touching their body, or having someone else get physically close to them or touch them.

*Ruth*

Ruth, a very pretty, petite 28-year-old woman, described her body as follows: "When I look at myself in the mirror, I see a grotesque monster. I see the wrinkles that are coming up in my face, my neck is like that of a turtle, my breasts are sagging, my stomach is huge, and my legs are flabby. My boyfriend says I have nothing to be ashamed of and quite a lot of other men pay me compliments about my appearance, but that doesn't make the slightest bit of difference to how I feel about myself. When I have a bath, I lock the door so that nobody can come in and see me. I undress and wash quickly; I can't stand being naked. It is too painful. I can't bear my boyfriend near me, let alone have him touch me. We haven't made love in months. I used to like pretty clothes, but now I just dress in big baggy jumpers to hide myself. I used to be a keen Morris dancer, but lately I couldn't face going any more. I can't bear the thought of all that loose flab wobbling around."

Perhaps you don't react quite as strongly as this. A specific trigger may make a person feel bad about their body, like a slight weight gain, or a feeling of premenstrual bloatedness, or for someone to make a remark related to your appearance.

*Felicity*

"I went to work wearing a new pullover. A colleague—whom I really like, said what a nice pullover I had. I immediately thought he meant "nice pullover on the wrong woman" and that he must have noticed how flat-chested I am. For the next three days I couldn't get rid of that thought. I have since avoided talking to him."

*Barbara*

"I often have people shouting nasty things after me as I walk along the road. I do absolutely nothing to provoke it. Most recently I walked past a building site. As I could see some men working there I crossed the road. They whistled and tried to get my attention. I just looked straight ahead, as if I hadn't heard anything. Then one of them shouted, "She's got a fat bum". They all laughed. Whenever something like that happens, it just brings out all my insecurities about my physical appearance, I feel totally unattractive. If people you don't know bother to make comments like that about you, it must mean there is some truth in it, mustn't it?"

But even if you encounter stresses, tensions, or unpleasant events that are nothing to do with your appearance—say, your boss criticises your work or you have a burst pipe in your flat—you may still respond by feeling bad about your body. For many eating disorder sufferers the way they feel about their body is the most sensitive barometer of how they feel about themselves and their life in general at a given point in time.

## LEARNING ABOUT BODY SHAPES

- Go to your local art/archaeological/anthropological museum or to a library. Look at pictures or statues of women. See how their shapes have changed over the centuries and how they differ across cultures. Get some postcards of ancient Greek or Roman statues or of African tribal women. Pin them up above your bed. What do they make you feel?
- Go into a cafe and watch passers-by. Find someone who isn't slim like a fashion model and who you still think looks good. What does it depend on whether you think someone looks good? Their style of dress? Their posture? Their facial expression? Anything else?

- Start with one inch of your body towards which you can be tender. Allow yourself to pamper this part, e.g. rub in some cream or massage it. Gradually increase the area that you can treat in this way.

## GETTING TO KNOW YOUR BODY

- Look at yourself naked in a full-length mirror. Look closely from head to toe; don't forget your ears and the soles of your feet. Take a hand-mirror to look at your back. What do you see? Write down three things you like about your body and three things you don't like about your body. Don't let yourself get away with not finding anything nice to say about yourself.
- Write down three things a close friend (male/female) and a stranger (male/female) might like about your appearance and three things they might not like.
- Close your eyes and touch and stroke your body, starting with your face, moving downwards, making sure you get a good feel of all the different parts. What do you feel? Is your skin rough or smooth, warm or cold, do you feel your heart beating, your ribcage move when you breathe, and your tummy rumble? Is it pleasurable or unpleasant or even frightening to do this?
- Stand against a wall. Press shoulders and head back firmly against it. What do you feel?
- Walk around as if you were very proud of your body, with your head upright. Make sure not to overstretch head or neck, as this will lead to neck ache and tension. (Walk as if you were suspended from a string).
- Put on your favourite slow piece of music and dance gently and quietly; now switch to your favourite fast record or tape and dance as vigorously as you can, and then relax.

## LOOKING AFTER YOUR BODY

If you don't like your body, you are likely to neglect it, to be out of tune with its rhythms, and to ignore its signals. Here are some suggestions as to how nurture it:

- Make sure you are getting enough sleep at night. Allow yourself some breaks during the day. Don't drive yourself on constantly.
- Draw up a list of things that you can do with or for your body/appearance and that make you feel good. How about walking, cutting wood, sunbathing, swimming, digging the garden, dancing, having a haircut, having a massage, soaking in aromatic oils? (If your list contains mainly vigorous sporting activities, think whether you are actually enjoying these things or whether they just make you feel good because they might make you lose weight.)

- Relaxation is another excellent way to recharge body and mind. The aim is to experience a state that lies between normal, day-to-day consciousness and sleep. If you liken your mind to a car, you want to achieve the state in which it is idling, in neutral, out of gear. There are several techniques for doing this, and some will suit you better than others, so try them all. Do not expect them to be easy or to produce magical solutions instantly. Like any skill (cycling, swimming, etc.), you need to practise regularly to master it.

Even with regular practice, some people find it quite difficult to achieve a state of relaxation. A relaxation tape can be a useful aid. You can make your own, by simply recording the instructions for the exercise below.

### Relaxation Exercise 1 [1]
This exercise is based on Progressive Relaxation Training, a method of learning to induce a state of physical "relaxation" by tensing and relaxing groups of muscles in a systematic way. Find a comfortable chair to sit in. Loosen any tight clothing, take off glasses if you wear them, and ensure that you are warm enough. You are now ready to begin.

- Close your eyes and concentrate on your breathing. Take a deep breath in, hold it, and breathe out. Then repeat. Take a deep breath in, hold it, and breathe out. Keep your breathing rhythm steady. Do not breathe so fast that you get lightheaded. During the relaxation exercise you will be asked to tense and relax various muscles; you will find it easier to breathe in when tensing and breathe out when relaxing.
- Screw up your eyes as tightly as possible, clench your teeth, and purse your lips. Feel the muscles in your face tighten and then feel the tension fall away as you allow the muscles to relax. And again, as you breathe in, screw up your eyes tightly, clench your teeth, and purse your lips, and slowly breathe out as you allow your muscles to relax. Once more, tighten the muscles in your face and hold before slowly breathing out and letting the muscles relax.
- Keep breathing in a steady rhythm, and raise your shoulders to your ears. Allow your shoulders to fall as you breathe out. Repeat this twice more, feeling the tension in your neck and shoulders fall away.
- Now tighten your muscles in your upper arms like a strong person, and hold for a while before relaxing and breathing out. Tense the muscles in the upper arms, and feel how heavy they are when you relax them.
- Now clench your hands to make a fist, hold them for a while, and then relax. Again, make your hands into a fist, hold, and gently allow your fingers to uncurl.

- Take a deeper breath in, and feel the muscles in your chest and stomach being expanded. Hold and slowly breathe out. Repeat this deeper breath in, hold it, and breathe out. Allow your breathing to return to its gentle rhythmic pattern.
- Now tighten the muscles of your stomach, and gradually breathe out as you relax them. Again, pull in your stomach muscles, hold, and relax. Once more, tense your stomach muscles, hold, and relax as you breathe out.
- Now work the muscles on your lower back and buttocks. Tighten them, hold, and relax. And repeat this a further two times.
- As you take your next breath in, tighten the muscles in your upper legs. Keep the tension for a while, and then relax as you exhale. Tense this set of muscles twice more.
- Now point your toes up towards your body, and tense the muscles in your calves. Hold, and then allow your muscles to relax. Repeat this once more. Your legs and feet should now feel heavy.
- Continue to breathe evenly. Your body now feels relaxed and comfortable and is sinking into the chair with heaviness. Allow your mind to drift with pleasant thoughts.
- End the relaxation exercise by slowly opening your eyes and gradually moving your body, becoming aware of your surroundings. You will now be feeling calm, refreshed, relaxed, and awake.
- Practise this exercise two or three times a day. Once you feel you have mastered it, gradually reduce the groups of muscles you use until a state of relaxation can be induced by mental means with minimal muscle exercise.


*Relaxation Exercise 2*
- Close your eyes and start by taking a deep breath in, hold it, and gently breathe out. And again breathe in, hold, and slowly breathe out. Keep your breathing steady throughout this exercise.
- Imagine that your body is full of fine, soft sand and that you have small holes in your fingertips and toes. The sand gradually leaves your body through your toes and fingers. Feel the sand filter out of your body, and, as it does so, feel your body become limp and heavy.
- Allow your head to drop forward as the sand starts to leave your body. As the level drops, your arms and abdomen feel heavy and limp and sink into the back of the chair. You can feel the sand draining slowly from your legs and, as it does, the muscles in your legs feel relaxed and limp. As the final grains of sand fall from your toes, your whole body feels relaxed, comfortable, and heavy. Keep your eyes closed and your breathing slow and steady and allow your mind to drift away

with pleasant and peaceful thoughts. When you wish to end the relaxation exercise, gradually open your eyes and become aware of your surroundings. Gradually move your arms and legs. You will now be feeling calm, refreshed, relaxed, and awake.

## LIVING WITH YOUR BODY

Living with/inside a body you don't like is difficult. Many of the people we see avoid getting on with their lives: they don't go out, they shelve having relationships, and ... and ... and ... . They all dream the same dream. "If only I ... —were slimmer, less pear-shaped, had thinner thighs, not such a big tummy, etc., my life would be completely different." Some people waste years like this.

Tragically, in the early phase of an eating disorder, some people achieve their ideal appearance for a short while through following a punishingly hard diet, and often this is remembered years later as the one good period in their life that they want to go back to at all cost. Only rarely do people allow themselves to remember how high the price they paid was.

*June*
"If I am honest with myself, it wasn't all rosy when I weighed seven stone. I thought about food day and night. I dreamt about it. I sometimes had nightmares about being force-fed. I felt guilty about absolutely anything I ate, I couldn't even eat an apple without regretting it. I remember having lots of arguments with my boyfriend. I think I was very irritable then. I lost my interest in music. Although a lot of people commented on how pretty I looked, my closest friends seemed to think I had undergone a complete personality change. I kept getting distracted, I couldn't concentrate, and I couldn't look at them when they talked to me. They didn't like it at all."

Women with eating disorders tend to overestimate the size of their body, the more out of control your eating is, the worse this gets. Working on your eating behaviour, therefore, will have a positive effect on your attitudes to your body. However, attitudes are much more difficult to change than behaviour, and they change much more slowly. So, even if you manage to get into a pattern of eating normally fairly quickly, your negative body image is likely to persist for a while longer. Be patient. You can't change everything overnight.

What you can do, however, is to work on those things you avoid due to feeling bad about your body. What is the point of wasting more time?

*Susan*

Susan made a list of all the things that she avoided. She wrote them down in hierarchical order, starting with the situations she feared most, progressing to the ones she feared least but still avoided. Here is her list:

- going swimming / to the beach in a bikini (impossible)
- dancing a slow dance with a man (very difficult to get physically close to someone)
- going to a party (difficult to meet new people and to know what to talk about)
- going to a restaurant with friends (worried what they will think about me if they see me eat)
- wearing tight skirts (worried about my stomach and lack of waist)
- wearing short sleeved T-shirts (because my arms are flabby)
- wearing brightly coloured clothes (fear this would draw attention to me)

- Make a similar list for yourself. Tackle an easy situation over the next week and a slightly more difficult one the week after. Include working on this in your weekly goals.

If you go ahead with this, don't expect to find it easy or to enjoy yourself at all initially. Expect to have a difficult, anxious, and very self-conscious time. It will take quite a bit of time before you can hope to feel more at ease with yourself. Getting better is about taking some risks. What do you have to lose?

## NOTE

1. Adapted from Wanigaratne, S., Wallace, W., Pullin, J., Keaney, F., & Farmer, R. (1990). *Relapse Prevention for Addictive Behaviours*. London: Blackwell Scientific Publications.

## FURTHER READING

Baker, N.C. (1984). *The Beauty Trap*. London: Piatkus.

Hutchinson, M.G. (1985). *Transforming Body Image*. Freedom, CA: Crossing Press.

Wolf, N. (1991). T*he Beauty Myth*. London: Vintage.

CHAPTER SEVEN

# Jack Spratt's Wife: Being Fatter May be Better

This chapter was written especially for those of you who, in addition to bulimia, have a problem with your weight, i.e. if your weight is above the top end of the weight band given for your height (in Table 3.1, chapter 3), you should definitely read this chapter.

Do you remember the nursery rhyme about Jack Spratt and his wife? "Jack Spratt could eat no fat, his wife could eat no lean ... ." She is usually portrayed as fat, but happy.

In our society, it is hard to be rounded and happy. Long gone are the days of Rubens and large actresses like Marilyn Monroe and Jane Russell. If you are within the heavy half of the population, you will be put under constant pressure to go on a diet. Magazines, newspapers, acquaintances, and even your friends may make you feel morally inferior unless you try to do something to conform to society's idealised norms.

*Josie*

"I was a big child, and a big teenager. I weigh 18 stone now. I have had years of comments, abuse, and humiliation because of it. It is amazing anybody feels they have the right to tell me off because of it. The other day I went to a new GP because of an ear-ache. He briefly dealt with my ear and then gave me a long lecture on the health risks of being overweight, and then he sent me off to see a dietician." Josie also noticed: "As long as I try to lose weight, others will be pleased with me, and I will get encouragement. If I ever eat a piece of cake in public, people comment: "Oh, I thought you were on a diet? Aren't you a bit naughty? Think of how nice you could look if you lost a bit of weight." Even if they don't say anything, I can see the disapproval in their faces. I can see they think, "she's letting herself go."

David Garner, one international authority, recently commented on the plight of the obese: "obesity is still one of the most stigmatized physical attributes in Western society today, leading to discrimination in a wide range of settings." He also commented that "It is time for greater emphasis on acceptance of fatness and concentration on the civil rights of the obese, with efforts at public education to counter the social stigmatization associated with fatness."

In 1992 in the United States, women's groups started to rebel against the diet dictators and began to smash weighing scales with the slogan, "Scales are for fish, not women".

## THE HEALTH RISKS OF BEING OVERWEIGHT

A powerful message to people who are heavy is that they are damaging their health, and many diets are started upon medical recommendation. Public health campaigns have emphasised that obesity is linked to heart disease, high blood pressure, diabetes, joint problems, and even certain sorts of cancer. However, scientists now think that the seriousness of these risks has been exaggerated, certainly for people who are only mildly or moderately overweight. Being plump may actually protect you against some forms of disease. Newer research also has shown that it is not high weight, as such, but your weight yo-yoing up and down—as is common for many people who regularly diet—that may lead to heart disease and even death. People who are heavy and fit probably don't have more health risks than those who are thinner.

## PIE IN THE SKY

You may say, "that's all very well, but I can't wait till society is more accepting of the kind of figure I have. I do want to lose weight." You will remember from chapter 3 that diets don't work. Any diet will increase the odds of you starting to binge eat. Your weight will begin to bounce up and down. This instability will lead to harmful metabolic patterns, with swings of insulin, fat, and sugar, and ultimately to your weight creeping up more and more. Thus a diet begun to improve health and beauty will have the opposite effect.

*Samantha*

Samantha, a 23-year-old beautician, gained over 6 stone in weight during a three year-period, which had started as a stringent diet and then progressed into the yo-yo cycle of binge eating, with her weight gradually going up and up. See Figure 7.1

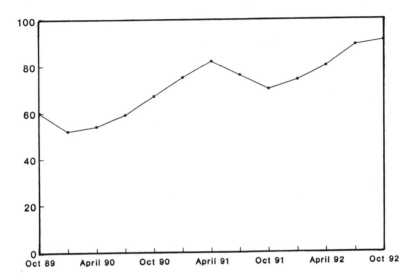

FIG. 7.1. Samantha's weight chart.

So the painful truth is that you really have to stop dieting to get over binges and to allow your weight to settle to a level that is right for you. To face up to this is extremely difficult. Monitoring your eating pattern by means of a diary, as we have introduced earlier, is an essential first step. It is important to structure your daily intake into meals and snacks.

*Alison*

Alison, a 24-year-old woman, found it impossible to control her eating. She would diet for one or two days and then spend the rest of the week bingeing. Her therapist told her that she must eat three meals a day plus three snacks, and that she could eat anything she wanted. "I was amazed. I realised that I had not been eating what I wanted for nearly all my adult life. I had been going from one diet to another, and here I was being told to eat regularly, and to eat anything I wanted, including potatoes, puddings, and sweets. I was totally surprised when after a week of doing this I had lost three kilos. I did not go on losing weight, but I managed to maintain my weight, which was the first time I had done that for almost as long as I could remember. After a couple of months, when I was really comfortable with eating regularly, my therapist suggested that it might be safe for me to cut down slightly. The way I did this was to make sure that I did not eat much more than 1700 calories a day. All that meant, really, was that I did not have huge great portions of anything, but I could continue eating all my favourite foods".

## ONLY THE LONELY

Because of the stigma of being fat, secondary problems can arise with your daily life-style, career, social and family life and contribute to the downward spiral. You may have put your life completely on "hold", not wanting to have any form of pleasure or enjoyment while you are fat. Subjecting yourself to loneliness and misery because of what you think others will say is a sure recipe for disaster and will ensure that you keep slipping further over the edge. It is therefore important that you begin to set goals and structure your life to take this into account.

*Samantha*

Samantha, whom we introduced to you earlier in this chapter, was so upset by her weight gain that she stopped working as a beautician, as she felt very inferior to the other girls with whom she worked and she could not fit into her uniform. She restricted her social life more and more and only left home to go shopping by car. She felt miserable and alone. With encouragement from her therapist, Samantha decided that she would try to go out and socialise at least once a week, although the thought of this terrified her. The next week Samantha reported back to her therapist: "I did it. I went out to the pub. I was absolutely terrified, and when I got there I felt that everyone was looking at me, seeing how fat, ugly, and horrible I was. I went with my friend, and we sat at a corner table, but, do you know, after about ten minutes or so I had totally forgotten about everyone staring at me and I was able to relax and enjoy myself. I really had a lovely evening, and I am going to go out again next week."

## SHAKE, SHAKE, SHAKE YOUR BODY

You may always have been someone who hated sport at school or who was laughed at, or ridiculed, for performing badly. You may be put off exercising because you feel you are not the right shape or size, and, like Samantha, you may want to hide away and isolate yourself from society.

Don't! You are not too fat to exercise. The variety of activities available to you is immense, and you can try different ones to find whatever is right for you. Regular exercise will probably not decrease your weight in a big way, but it can increase your metabolic rate and enable your weight to remain stable. Contrary to common belief, exercise does not increase appetite but slightly decreases it. Exercise also increases suppleness, strength, and stamina. It is an ideal method of dealing with stress. It can take your mind off your problems, and after a session of exercise you will feel warm, comfortable, and relaxed. It can thus replace overeating or purging, which, for many people with eating disorders, are their prime ways of coping with stress. Exercise can also lift depression and help sleep.

Remember:

1. Exercise can burn off calories.
2. It promotes health.
3. It can give you a sense of mastery, and so help you deal with stress.
4. It helps your weight to stabilise rather than go up.
5. It preserves body muscle.

## Overcoming Obstacles

- The type of "all-or-nothing" approach to life that many people with eating disorders have means that they jump in at the deep end and do something to excess, which is painful and uncomfortable and then is not repeated. It is much better to start with something that you enjoy and build up the intensity slowly and gradually. It should not have to hurt to do you good. If it does you are pushing yourself too hard. If your breathing is uncomfortable, slow down.
- The need to please others and a fear of being selfish, which are other characteristics of people with eating disorders, may lead you to think that you have not got time to devote to something that is primarily for yourself. You do not need that much time. Just 20 minutes, two to three times per week, can be sufficient, and you may then find that, with practice, it becomes easy to put aside the time.
- Even if you have young children, you can probably find a way of getting more exercise. Many sport and leisure centres now have child-care facilities, and you can get details of these from your local Council Leisure and Recreation Department or your local library.
- Try to incorporate your children into your exercise schedule if possible, as this will set up good habits for them. You can take them in a pushchair when you go for long walks, or you can put them on your bicycle.
- Perhaps you could think of doing something that involves someone else. Could you persuade a friend to join you at a club or a class?

- Try to choose something that fits into your routine easily, so you can do it regularly. Don't take on something for which you have to travel far or that you can only do under certain weather conditions.
- The self-defeating "toad-in-the-hole" outlook on life (described in chapter 10) makes many people who are overweight avoid any form of exercise, as they fear that they will look ridiculous or that others will mock and jeer at them. Although there will always be an ignorant minority who think this way, people whose view you would respect would commend your enterprise and your bravery in facing a challenge and doing something positive rather than avoiding the problem.
- If you have a medical condition such as a heart problem or a muscle problem or simply are worried about whether exercise is right for you, go and discuss it with your general practitioner. There are, however, very few people for whom moderate exercise is dangerous.

## How to Change Your Lifestyle to Get Fitter!

We need to repeat that an "all-or-nothing" or an "either I am perfect or I am useless" approach to life are totally out of place in the context of exercise. You do not have to start marathon running! An increase in mobility and stamina can be achieved by slight changes in your lifestyle through more walking and increased activity around your house and work.

The way to do it is to find more active ways of doing the things you usually do. Don't save things up to be efficient, do them as you think of them.

### Walking

This is excellent and is available to all, with few risks of injury or strain. You can use your time whilst walking to observe, to think, to listen to music or a radio, to learn a language or to talk with a friend.

Apart from reasonably comfortable shoes, you do not need expensive equipment. To prepare yourself, put talcum powder on your feet (and tights), and afterwards persuade a friend to give you a foot massage or have a ten-minute soak in the bath with some aromatic oil in it.

Begin walking for 15 minutes each day, increasing by 5 minutes each day or week. If the 15-minute walk is too difficult, go for a shorter period initially. The goal should be to walk one hour each day.

By the way, walking burns off the same number of calories as running the same distance. How far you go is more important than how fast you go.

Think of ways of including walking in your life:

- Get up 30 minutes early to walk.
- Walk during lunch breaks.
- Walk after work.
- Walk before bed.

Experiment to find the best combination of place, time, and companionship for you.

Walking with a partner can be an excellent time for talking together without the distractions of television or newspaper. It can give you both time to unwind and to mull things over. You do not need to have a dog to have a regular walk around the block!

Try to include walking in your every-day pattern of life, but there is no need to despair if you miss the odd day. Try to plan your holidays with this in mind.

*Using Stairs*
Climbing stairs burns more calories per minute than do vigorous activities like jogging and cycling. It is very easy to incorporate the use of stairs into your lifestyle, because you can find stairs at home, at work, in shops, and on public transport, etc. In modern buildings it may take some detective work to find the stairs, but they will be there. One large American study by Dr Ralph Paffenbarger from Stanford University found that people who climbed only 50 stairs (not flights) each day had a reduced risk of heart attack.

Avoid using the lift whenever possible, or take it to the floor below where you have to go, so that you walk up the last flight. Use every opportunity to go up and down the stairs at home or at work. Try to ensure that you have to use stairs to go to the toilet or to make a drink.

Measuring Your Goals
The pulse test is a simple means of measuring your progress with exercise. Time your pulse every month. As you get fitter, your pulse rate in response to exercise should decrease. The pulse rate in untrained people is usually about 80 beats per minute.

How to do it: Wrap the fingers of one hand around the back of the other wrist. Press the index and middle finger on the upturned wrist until you can feel the pulsing of blood through the vessel. Count the number of beats in exactly 15 seconds.

Multiply the number by 4 to calculate your beats per minute. Take your pulse rate both at rest and during exercise.

If you want to get guidance on how to increase your activity, write to the Health Education Council to get a copy of their booklet "Exercise, Why Bother?" You can get it for free if you write to:

Publications Section
Health Education Authority
Hamilton House
Mabledon Place
London WC1H 9TX

Here is how some people with eating disorders have increased their exercise:

*Samantha*

Samantha was initially very pessimistic about trying to increase her exercise as she had tried to go to an aerobics class that she had attended before she had gained weight. Samantha was terribly upset to find that she could not keep up with even the easiest exercises in the class. Her therapist explained that she needed to start exercising very gradually, and, between them, they decided that ten minutes' brisk walking a day was all that Samantha should aim at. "When my therapist suggested ten minutes' walking a day, I thought that was absolutely hopeless. I felt that I ought to be exercising really, really hard for hours and hours or not bother to do anything at all. My therapist explained that my body would take time to readjust to exercise and that it was best to build up gradually. I was not really convinced, but I thought that I would go along with it as I had been so upset that I could not do the aerobics. What I started doing was go out for a walk in the evening with my friend when I felt that it had got a bit dark and people would not be likely to see me. We would walk for a little bit, and then I would say that it was time to do my ten minutes' brisk walking, so I would really increase the speed for ten minutes, and then we would slowly walk back to the house. I soon found that this was less of a challenge, and gradually I began to build up the amount of time I was spending walking briskly by five minutes each week. Just going out of the house made me feel less sensitive about people seeing me, and I started going out for walks during the daytime as well. It gave me such a good feeling to realise that I was doing something positive about my problem and not just sitting, waiting for it to go away."

*Claire*

Claire was a 29-year-old woman who found it very difficult to get any exercise as she worked as a telephonist and spent all of her day sitting down. "I just really did not know how I would get any exercise and fit it into my day. Then I had the idea of getting off the bus one stop early and walking that last little bit to work. I was amazed how exhausted it made me feel the first few days I tried it. It did get easier, though, and really my perseverance paid off, and I began getting off the bus two stops earlier, then three stops, and now a year and a half later I am cycling to work. I feel so virtuous when I cycle past the bus and see all these pasty faces in the window and think that used to be me."

## Some Exercises to Do at Home

Lots of people prefer to exercise at home. It's private, and there's no need to get a babysitter or travel anywhere. However, you might get more out of it if you go to a class first and learn how to do the exercises properly. Below we describe six simple stretching exercises. Do them at least three times a week, and you'll begin to feel your body becoming more supple and relaxed. You should also do them to warm up before starting on anything more vigorous. Do all stretching exercises slowly and smoothly. Repeat each one 8 to 12 times. Doing them more times or more quickly won't have any extra benefit. You don't need to do 12 on the first day. Just do as many as you are comfortable doing, and gradually build up. If you have trouble with back pain, it might be advisable to see your doctor first. In any case, do these exercises very gently.

*Arm Circling:* This is to maintain suppleness in your shoulders.

- Stand tall and relaxed, with your arms at your sides. Slowly circle your right shoulder backwards. Repeat with your left shoulder, and continue on alternate sides.
- Place your right hand on your right shoulder. Move your elbow forwards, up, and back, in a circle. Repeat with your left elbow, and continue on alternate sides.
- Start with your arms straight at your sides. Keep your hips facing forwards, and move your right arm forward, up, and back, to form a large circle. Repeat on the left, and continue on alternate sides.
  Any of these arm circles can be done with both arms together.

*Forward Bending:* This is to stretch the muscles in your shoulders, trunk, and legs.

- Stand tall and relaxed. Stretching through your whole body, reach up towards the ceiling with your fingertips. Then, letting yourself bend at the hips and the knees, slowly bring your hands down towards the floor as far as is comfortable. Straighten up, and repeat.

*Side Bending:* This is to stretch the muscles in your sides and help keep your spine flexible.

- Stand tall and relaxed, with your feet apart and hands at your sides. Slowly bend to the left and right alternately, allowing your hands to slide down the sides of your legs. Stand tall in-between bends. Keep your legs straight. Make sure you are bending to the side and not letting your shoulders drop forwards. Move only as far as you can comfortably, and return to the upright position. Don't bounce into the movement.

*Leg Swinging:* This is to keep your hips mobile and to stretch the thigh muscles.

- Stand tall and relaxed, with your weight on your left leg. Rest your left hand on the back of a chair for support if necessary. Now swing your right leg forwards and backwards in a relaxed pendulum action. Gradually take your leg as high as you comfortably can, keeping your body fairly upright and letting your right knee bend. Repeat with your left leg.

*Calf Stretching:* This is to stretch your calves and keep your ankles mobile.

- Stand facing a wall at arm's length from it. Place your hands on the wall for support, and stretch your right leg out straight behind you, with the ball of your foot on the floor and your toes pointing towards the wall. Gently push your right heel towards the floor, allowing your left leg to bend as necessary.

*Ankle Reaching:* This is to stretch your lower back and the backs of your thighs.

- Sit on the floor, with your legs straight in front of you and your knees as near to the floor as is comfortable. Place your hands on top of your thighs. Slowly and smoothly slide your hands down your legs as far as you can comfortably reach. Return to the upright position, and repeat. Do not bounce into the movement.

## Venturing Out

*Swimming:* This is good for increasing strength, stamina, and suppleness. It is particulary good if you are heavy or have some disability, as your body is supported by the water and there is no strain on your joints. Many local swimming pools have special sessions for women only or women with toddlers. There are often cheap rates, or you can buy a season ticket. Get in touch with your local authority leisure department.

*Susan*

Susan had always been heavy, but after the birth of her child her eating pattern became chaotic, and her weight increased. She had always been quite active, but as she became more ashamed of her body, she went out less. When it was suggested to her that she take up swimming, she was very reluctant. She said she would be ashamed to take her clothes off in public. However, she went to see what was available at her local swimming pool and leisure centre. They did not have sessions for women only, but they did have early-morning sessions, so she decided to go to these first thing and wear a long T-shirt over her bathing costume. She found that, at that time of day, most people at the pool were sleepy and preoccupied and did not notice her. She was thus able to go three times a week before her husband left for work.

*Margaret*

Margaret had always been in the top half of the normal range of weight. Diabetes ran in her family, and during her pregnancy she became mildly diabetic. After the birth of her child it disappeared. She was, however, concerned that if she did nothing about her weight, she would run a high risk of developing diabetes. She knew that she should exercise more. Her doctor had told her that swimming would be a good form of exercise. However, she felt that she would be unable to stretch her budget enough to visit the local swimming pool frequently, and so, with the help of her doctor, she started to mount a small campaign. Here is the letter she sent to the director of leisure at her local council, to the counsellors for her area, to the managers of the swimming pools, to her local MP, and to the Secretaries of State for Health and Social Services:

*Dear ......,*

*I have a problem with my weight, and it is putting my health at risk. In the 1992 Government White Paper, Health of the Nation, one of the target areas is to reduce obesity within the UK. Exercise is recognised as being a good way of promoting health and for getting control over weight, and the Health Education Council has written a pamphlet suggesting that we do more exercise.*

*I would therefore like to go swimming, the form of exercise recommended by my doctor for me. There are, however, two problems that prevent me from doing this:*

*1. I cannot afford to go swimming on a regular basis.*
*2. I am frightened and intimidated when I do go.*

*Is it not possible to have free swimming for those who are unable to pay and whom doctors recommend a change in their lifestyle?*

*Also, would it be possible to have special sessions dedicated to people like me, who are overweight or who have some other form of disability?*

*I would be prepared to come and discuss this with you if necessary.*

*Thank you for your help*

*Margaret Miller*

Once you have become more active, you may want to diversify your exercise programme.

*Cycling:* This is good for stamina and leg strength. It is possible to get second-hand bikes, and they are easy to maintain. You can cycle safely in local parks or join a club.

*Jogging and Running:* This is popular, but you can develop overuse injury to your lower limbs, so try to run on soft surfaces and with good shoes. You can join clubs, and these do not only cater for high performers.

*Golf:* Some local authorities have public courses that are reasonably priced.

*Bowling:* This is a sociable sport, and clubs are growing with recruits of all ages.

*Racket Sports:* Some, like badminton, are good for beginners and can be played at evening classes or local clubs.

*Weight Training:* More and more women are entering into this, but you should learn how to do it safely by joining a class at your local leisure centre.

*Martial Arts and Judo:* Many clubs are available, but make sure that they belong to the national governing body.

*Exercise Classes (Yoga, Movement and Dance):* Make sure that the class is at the right level. Start off with a beginners' class. It is important that you get on with the teacher—not everybody will—so you may need to change classes.

## FURTHER READING

Bovey, S. (1989). *Being fat is not a sin*. London: Pandora.

Donald, C. (1987). *The fat woman measures up*. Charlottetown, Canada: Rageweed Press.

Harper, A., & Lewis, G. (1982). *The big beauty book*. New York: Holt, Reinhart & Winston.

Lyons, P., & Burgard, D. (1990). *Great shape: First fitness guide for large women*. Palo Alto, CA: Bull Publishing Co.

Nichols, G. (1984). *The fat black woman's poems*. London: Virago

Olds, R. (1984). *Big & beautiful*. Washington, DC: Acropolis Books

Palmer, A. (1985). *You fat slob*. London: Futura.

Roberts, N. (1985). *Breaking all the rules*. New York: Viking.

Weldon, F. (1982). *The fat woman's joke*. London: Hodder & Stoughton.

Wersba, B. (1987). *Fat: A love story*. London: Bodley Head.

# CHAPTER EIGHT

# Relapse: Walking In Circles—Or Not

Your eating disorder will remain your Achilles' Heel for the rest of your life, and it will be there to trip you up when you least expect it. You need to know how to prevent slips from occurring and what to do if a slip occurs.

## PREVENTING SLIPS FROM OCCURRING

### Plan Your Own Relapse

Every single person recovering from an eating disorder has to face numerous set-backs before the eating problem fades into the background. Knowing this can help you not to panic too much about the prospect of having a slip. Many sufferers find, once they haven't binged and vomited for a while, that they get increasingly panicky and worried that a set-back might strike any day now and might hit them harder then ever (Do you recognise this as an irrational belief ? You will find more on this subject in chapter 10). One practical way of dealing with this panic is to have a planned relapse. No, we are not having you on: bringing on, deliberately, what you fear most is an excellent way of getting on top of your fears.

- Set aside some time, buy your favourite binge foods, and have a binge. Spread all the food out on the table, and eat as much of it as you can. Concentrate on your binge as fully as you can. Can you bring yourself to stuff it down as you always used to? Can you bring yourself to eat similar amounts as you always used to? How does it feel? Is it really the worst thing that could ever happen to you? Having done this, do you feel you are back to square one?

• Repeat this exercise at least once a month if you are worried that you are doing too well.

## WHAT TO DO IF A SLIP OCCURS

Don't make a mountain out of a molehill. Don't damn yourself. After you have slipped, your automatic thoughts will be to "awfulise" the event and to damn yourself. You may believe that if you slip once, you are a total failure and will never be able to get better. You may tell yourself that changing is too hard, and the discomfort of trying and failing and trying again is too much to bear.

It is important for you to try to argue yourself out of the illogicality of these statements. Consider the temptation to binge and vomit as a trial. You win some, and you lose some. One loss does not mean that you will fail next time.

### Learning from Slips

Try to stand back from how you feel about your lapse, and take a cool critical look at how it actually came about. Don't say it just happened. There is always a reason. Ask yourself the following questions:

• Have you gone against any of the dietary ground-rules outlined in chapter 3? Have you allowed yourself to eat enough at mealtimes? Have you omitted meals or left long gaps between them?

• Is bingeing still the easiest and quickest way of getting pleasure in your life? If so, you will need to change your life so that there are other ways of getting pleasure that do not lead to long-term problems.

• Was your lapse caused by stress, upset, unhappiness, anxiety, or any other unpleasant feeling? If so, what other ways of dealing with these triggers do you have?

The more carefully you think about your lapse, the more it can teach you and can help you to make different plans, either to stop getting tempted or to cope differently if temptation arises. Don't just ignore a slip and rely on your willpower to change. Take active steps to change the behaviour and situations that act as triggers, and get others to help make these changes. If you do slip once, you can still decide whether you are going to continue to binge eat and have a complete relapse or whether you are going to stop the episode.

# A WOMAN'S WORK IS NEVER DONE—OR IS IT?

Many women, and especially women with an eating disorder, devote the majority of their time to caring for other people's needs, whether at work, within the family, or within their social network, and they have difficulties looking after their own needs, or even recognising that they have needs and wants. An imbalance between shoulds, those activities that you see as chores or things you feel obliged to do, and "wants", those activities carried out for pleasure, is often responsible for relapse. "Shoulds" and "wants" are subjective, depending on pressures and circumstances. Table 8.1 shows the diary of one of our patients, Isabel, a young solicitor.

You can see that most of Isabel's day was made up of "shoulds". The only "wants" she allowed into her day were food-related, and these were all concentrated at the end of the day. Do you recognise this? Does food, when you allow yourself to have it, give you this much of a thrill? Often women with eating disorders find it difficult to give up overeating, as this constitutes the only thrill or pleasure in their life (and the one pleasure that is most easily accessible).

- Draw up your own "shoulds" and "wants" diary for a week.
- Are you the sort of person who allows the "shoulds" to take over your life? You need to create a balance in your life and to ensure that you

TABLE 8.1
Isabel's "shoulds" and "wants" Diary

| Activity | Should | Want |
|---|---|---|
| Get up | + | |
| Drive to work | + | |
| Deal with mail & phone calls | + | |
| 3 appointments | + | |
| Running late, no time for lunch | + | |
| Go to bank | + | |
| Writing reports | + | |
| 2 further clients | + | |
| Shop—buy biscuits & chocolate to eat in the car | | + + |
| Drive home | + | |
| Make self sick | | + |
| Tidy flat | + | |
| Iron clothes | + | |
| Finish reports for work | + | |
| Supper | | + |
| Binge | | + |

incorporate into it activities in which you look after yourself—both your mind and body.

- How could you make sure there is more balance in your life?
- What could you do to comfort and excite yourself, besides eating?
- Make a list of your "wants" and desires. Include big and small things on your list: wild, decadent dreams like "a three-week holiday in a luxury hotel in Barbados", and some simple things, like "ten minutes to myself every morning to do some relaxation". Make a start with the small things, and make sure you incorporate at least one of those into every day.

# CHAPTER NINE

# The Wounds
# of Childhood

Some of you will have been deprived of the safe, consistent loving and nurturing experience every child deserves. Problematic or inadequate parenting, with repeated arguments and violence amongst parents, physical abuse, and sexual abuse is common for sufferers of eating disorders. This can be the result of the parents splitting up or a parent dying, or it may stem from psychological problems in a parent, like depression or alcohol abuse.

In other cases the problems are less overt. Your parents may have had little time or energy for you, or they may have lacked interest in you, being physically or emotionally unavailable to you, perhaps because they were too preoccupied with their work or perhaps because they were depressed following the breakdown of their marriage. Or maybe they gave you the feeling that you would only be accepted if you were good, successful, or clever. Lack of approval and withheld affection can leave profound scars, with later difficulties in relationships.

*Sandra*

Sandra grew up in South Africa. Her parents split up when she was four. Her mother then remarried. The stepfather drank heavily. When he was drunk, he would beat Sandra and her two sisters or force them to drink whisky. There were incessant arguments between him and their mother. Sandra repeatedly witnessed her stepfather beating her mother. "We were terrified when they fought. I often feared he might kill my mother." Most of the time Sandra was left completely to her own devices. The family had several servants, one of whom forced Sandra to have sexual intercourse with him on several occasions. He threatened to kill her should she tell her parents. When Sandra was 12 years of age, her mother left the stepfather, and Sandra was sent to England to live with her natural father. "At first I wanted to live with him. In fact, when I still lived with my mother and stepfather I often dreamt that my father would come and rescue me. But once I was living with him, our relationship became quite fraught. He was pretty strict and tried to make me work for school. He often criticized me, the way I dressed, and my friends; he felt that I didn't work hard enough at school. I think he probably tried his best to get on with me, but I was pretty rebellious in my early teens, and I simply didn't trust him enough."

Such negative childhood experiences often produce low self-esteem, depression, suppressed anger, or open rebellion and difficulties in developing trusting relationships. Instead of adopting a "give-and-take" middle ground in your relationships, you may find yourself fluctuating between extreme positions where you either idealise people, putting them on a pedestal, or feel totally negative about them. This leads to loneliness or feeling let down or ignoring your own needs.

Do you recognise the following?

- Did you have to fend for yourself as your parents were absent or preoccupied; did you therefore have to grow up before your time?
- Were you ruled with an iron rod, with fear of violence to yourself or to others?—You may have been left feeling crushed or rebellious.
- Did you only feel loved if you came up to certain standards in looks, behaviour, or achievement?
- Do you feel that your parents were perfect? Were you and your parents best friends?—This may make it difficult for you to reach out and explore other relationships.
- Do you feel that you were envied? Did you have better chances than others?—This may make you deny and spoil your luck.
- Do you feel that your physical and emotional needs were neglected or damaged? Were you used as a scapegoat for your parents' feelings of anger or dissatisfaction?
- Draw your family tree.
- What are your memories of your early family life? Perhaps you can jot some things down. For example, how did your family deal with:
  - relatives
  - mealtimes/celebrations

- school/friends
- religion/authority figures
- money/talents/gifts
- illness/losses
- Write your life story, and put in events as suggested above, but also identify the abstract beliefs and motivations that underlay these events. Show your story to a friend.

## SEXUAL ABUSE

Sexual abuse in childhood is a form of trauma that may be particularly difficult to come to terms with because of the aura of secrecy and taboo that surrounds it.

### What is Sexual Abuse?

Child sexual abuse happens when an adult or older person touches or uses a child in a sexual way. This can include many different kinds of activities but the main thing is that, by being bigger, stronger, or having power or authority in the victim's life, the adult can trap, lure, force, or bribe them into sexual activity.

### *How Do I Know if I Have Been Sexually Abused?*
Here are some examples of the different things that can happen:

Being ...

- cuddled or kissed in a way that left you feeling uncomfortable
- bathed in a way that made you feel uneasy
- made to watch sexual acts or look at other people's genitals
- shown sexual films or videos, or being forced to listen to sexual talk
- made to pose for "sexual" photographs
- touched on your breasts or genitals
- made to touch an adult's or older person's genitals
- made to have oral sex
- penetrated (having the adult thrust a finger, his penis, or an object inside the vagina or anus)
- raped (penetrated using force or violence)

There are other, less obvious things that may have been done or said to you that you have found abusive.

### Why is it Wrong?
This form of early sexual activity is wrong because it hurts the victim, sometimes physically, but more often psychologically. We know that it can cause confusion, fear, anger, shame, self-blame and leave the victim

with a very poor opinion of themselves. Without help, the victim can sometimes have serious problems in later life.

It is wrong because everybody should have a right to decide what happens to their body. Adults should normally protect that right for children and young people, so any situation where physical force is used or threatened, or where the person feels they can't say no, can be called sexual assault. Children and young people, for many reasons, can't really say no to adults, nor have they the power to stop them. Young children do not even understand what is happening. The adult in this situation is always committing a crime. About 10% of women in the community and approximately 30 to 40% of women with eating disorders have been sexually abused in their childhood or raped in later life. The spectrum of abuse ranges from one-off experiences to repeated abuse over years. Any form of sexual abuse constitutes a gross exploitation of a power relationship. Often the abuser is a member of the family or someone known to the family.

## TRYING TO MAKE SENSE OF IT

Victims of sexual abuse commonly feel that they are to blame for what happened, that they allowed the abuse to happen or somehow provoked it. Physical force or psychological threats are often used to silence the victim and are designed to confuse you by making you feel as though you are in the wrong or as if you invited the advances. It is also common for a victim who is brave enough to discuss the abuse, to meet with disbelief, and the whole thing getting hushed up in the family. In many cases the perpetrator goes on living within the family or near-by.

*Hazel*

Hazel was sexually abused for a number of years by her father's brother, from when she was very young. She would often spend summer holidays with this uncle and his wife. "When my aunt was out doing the shopping, he would often ask me whether I wanted him to read a story. He then took me on his lap and began to touch me up, my genitals, my breasts. I could feel that he had an erection. I had a sense that this was wrong. I didn't ask him to stop. I didn't tell my parents at the time." Hazel eventually mustered up the courage to tell her parents about this when she was 16. "My mother was very good about it, but my father, I think, still doesn't believe me. He accused me of lying and got very cross with me. I think he was totally shocked that something like this could happen in his family. I never now go to see my uncle. My parents still go, because they wouldn't want open conflict in the family. I am really frightened that he could do it to someone else, too."

Many victims of sexual abuse feel that the abuse completely changed the way they feel about themselves as a person and that they have been left with a wound that will never heal. Kathy, another one of our patients, whose father repeatedly raped her when she was in her teens, said, "it feels like some poison is growing inside me".

- If you have been sexually abused it may seem too difficult to talk to someone about this at the moment—or you might decide you want to do something about it now.
- First, it will help if you read other sufferers' experiences of abuse. You will not feel so alone, full of shame and different to the rest of society.

At the end of this chapter you will find a reading list that may be of interest to you. Go to your local library, and order one of the books.

- You may want to talk to someone anonymously about it. Self-help lines are available (unfortunately they are often busy).
- Write down what happened to you, but as a story of a court scene, as if it had happened to someone else. Write down what the prosecuting lawyer for the victim would say. Here is the way he might set about it:
  - How did the abuse start?
  - Were there ways the abuser got you to keep it secret?
  - How long did it continue?
  - What were the worst things about it?
  - What did the abuser do?
  - Write down what the defence lawyer for the perpetrator would say.
  - Then write down the jury's response, and finally, the judge's speech.
- Could you show your story to anyone else? They may be able to help complete the lawyer's case, give more of the jury's verdict, and ensure that the judge was wise. If the victim of the story was your own child, would any of the arguments differ?

Trying to understand and make sense of what happened to you leads to confusing feelings, so try to answer these questions:

- Do you blame yourself for the abuse? Who else is to blame?
- Do you have secret fears about yourself? Or about others?
- If you are angry, what are you angry about?
- If you are scared, what are you scared about?
- It gets particularly confusing if you have some good memories and feelings about the abuser. This doesn't indicate that you are a monster. Children naturally try to see the good in things. What were the good memories? Do you have good memories you want to keep?
- Similarly, many victims are left with mixed feelings about their parents. What are your good and bad feelings towards your parents?

- Rank the strength of your feelings on a scale of 1 to 10.
- Draw yourself and other members of the family. See how you draw them and what feelings these drawings evoke in you.
- Record your feelings in your diary, and do the ABC detective work as outlined in chapter 2.

## The Right to be Angry

Anger is a natural response to abuse, but you may have learnt that getting angry leads to more abuse, or you may feel that anger is not what you are allowed to feel. You may have witnessed terrible violence done in anger and so think that it is necessary to suppress it.

The abuser often stifles or deflects the victim's anger and it is turned inwards, therefore you feel bad or you take your anger out on yourself by hurting yourself or deadening your anger with food. Is it fair to continue to add to the burden of hurt and pain carried by the child victim inside you?

## What Can You Do with Angry Feelings?

The first step is to recognise your anger and allow yourself a glimpse at it. You may need to spend 15 minutes quietly meditating, focusing on your anger. Listen to your body and its sensations. Give it time, and you may be able to answer all of the questions below.

- Who are you angry with?—The abuser? Your parent? Yourself? The world?
- Are you just annoyed or are you furious?
- Look at what you normally do with angry feelings:
  - Do you yell at people?
  - Do you tease and criticise?
  - Do you lash out?
  - Do you break things?
  - Do you hurt yourself?
  - Do you take your feelings out on someone else?
  - Do you keep them bottled up?
  - Do you tell people about them?
  - Do you do something to change what is making you angry?
  - Do you remain passive?
  - What have you done to express your anger in the past?
  - What would you like to do to show people that you are angry?
  - Do you ever secretly think about the things you would like to do to show your anger?

Here are some ways that have helped other people get their angry feelings about abuse out into the open. You might feel inhibited at first when you are trying them, but they often do work.

- Imagine a child you know or care about being treated in the same way you were treated.
- Read other victims' stories (see reading list)—perhaps you can feel angry for them.
- Go somewhere safe, and get into an angry posture—make angry faces, shout and swear, scream. Get a friend to scream with you!
- Try asking your supporter to sit in front of you and put up their palms facing you. Now push against them with your palms. Push hard. Get your supporter to push back. Get mad.
- Punch cushions. Hitting the bed with a tennis racket, or a rolled-up newspaper is just as good and makes a great noise.
- With your helper, act out situations which make you feel angry.

Make some rules about this—not hurting anyone else, not hurting yourself.

- Talk to your pillow/doll and explain why you are so angry. Sometimes venting your anger can make you aware of other kinds of feelings as a powerful aftermath—loneliness, sadness, and grief. It is a good idea to have someone around who understands what you are trying to do and can comfort you.

Here are some ideas for directly targeting your anger:

- Draw pictures of the abuser. Tell them what you would like to do to them. Tear them up into little pieces. Put them on the wall, and throw things at them.
- Make your own models of the abuser in clay or plasticine. Stick pins in them. Squash them. Break them into little pieces.
- Imagine the abuser in "the empty chair". If you can't say angry things to him, get your supporter to do it.
- Listen to family members, friends, or your helper being angry on your behalf.
- Make a list of the ways in which the abuse has affected you. You are bound to find things to be angry about.
- Write a letter to the person who abused you (even if the person is no longer around or even dead). You shouldn't send the letter. It is private—just for you. Write all your angry thoughts in it. Don't hold back. Call the abuser all the names you want. Describe how hurt you are and why.
- Try dictating the letter onto a tape-recorder.

- Re-read your letter, or play back your tape. Add some more before you put it somewhere safe.
- Or take out your letter, and rip it to shreds. Tear it into the smallest pieces possible.

Sometimes you can feel so much anger that is hard to talk without losing control. Try some physical exercise. Run, jog, take the dog for a walk. Try some aerobics. Jump up and down.

At some point or another you may have strong feelings of wanting to get back at the person who has hurt you. You dream of revenge—or even murder. Wanting revenge is a natural impulse, a sane response. Of course you can't act on it, but let yourself imagine it to your heart's content. That is one way of getting it out of your system.

Remember, being angry with someone doesn't cancel out the good feelings you might have about them. You have a right to your anger. Expressing it clears the way for you to feel whole again.

## GRAPPLE WITH GUILT AND SELF-BLAME

Many victims of abuse are plagued by the thought that they are to blame for what happened. You may be aware that part of you enjoyed what happened, or that you are to blame because you accepted bribes, or that simply by going along with the abuse you are somehow responsible for it.

NO, NEVER! No one has the right to abuse you sexually either by force or by abusing their position. It is never the victim's fault. The abuser is totally responsible for his own behaviour. It is never anything the victim does or says that causes the abuse. Equally, the victim is not responsible for what happens to the family or abuser after speaking out.

Do you torture yourself by telling yourself that:

- It was something about you that "invited" the abuse?
- You were the kind of person who "deserved" it?
- You enjoyed the special attention involved ... or the rewards ... or you accepted money?
- You "used" the secret to get some kind of advantage over the abuser?
- You experienced pleasurable physical feelings associated with the abuse?
- You didn't tell?
- You didn't do enough to stop the abuse?
- You didn't do enough to prevent brothers and sisters being abused?
- By telling, you have upset your family or brought them unwelcome attention?
- You are responsible for breaking up the family?
- You have brought punishment on the abuser?
- You have behaved in destructive or self-destructive ways?

Pretend your list belonged to someone else who has suffered abuse, and you were that person's friend. What would you say to them?

Often the abuse starts so early that you didn't know what was going on. Although you may have suspected that it wasn't quite right, by the time you knew that it was wrong it had been going on so long you felt you couldn't object or tell. Remember that children have to trust adults and can be confused easily, but always need affection and attention and so will join in any interaction with an adult. Sexual responses are instinctive and can develop at an early age.

## WILL THE EFFECTS ALWAYS BE THERE?

Different people are affected in different ways, and the after-effects of the abuse don't just depend on what happened, but on what help and support the victim has. Often abuse leads to difficulties that persist in adult life and with relationships with others. Once you realise how your abuse affects you, you can overcome it.

REMEMBER: EVERY VICTIM CAN BE A SURVIVOR!

## GET A TOEHOLD ONTO TRUST

After abuse of any sort, lack of trust is imprinted on your personality. When you can't trust, a vicious circle begins. The less you trust, the fewer friends you will have and the more isolated you become. You do not give yourself the opportunity to relearn that people can be trusted, you feel lonely and vulnerable and guard yourself more.

Going through life without trust is very lonely, so when you have the courage to try, take it slowly. You may have setbacks, but don't give up, the gains are great. You may find it helpful to read *The Little Prince* by Antoine De St. Exupery, who recognised that love involved the risk of being hurt but that a life bereft of friendships was no life. Trust will take time to develop—be patient. Eventually you will experience its components—honesty, acceptance, and respect. Beware of romantic myths, such as those portrayed in Mills & Boon novels, suggesting that there is only one man to be with in your life, or that a "Prince Charming" (strong, macho) will whisk you off your feet (in real life he may turn out to be a domineering brute).

It is often difficult to get the balance between caring and dependence right when you have not experienced such balance in your childhood. You may need to spend longer in the phase of developing friendships with women before you start relationships with men. It is better that you do make this work thoroughly, rather than risk entering into another victim/abuser relationship. Try to answer the following questions:

- Do you feel that, if you depend on someone, they are in charge, and you have to give in?
- Do you fear that getting close to someone will end up with you being hurt, and therefore you opt for the "lonely but in charge" road?
- Do you swing between feeling of contempt for others and the idea that they will ridicule or humiliate you?
- Do you swing between feeling a brute or a baby?

If any of these patterns ring true, go back to your family tree and family diagram.

- What are your family mottoes? Where do these myths come from?
- Re-write the story in the same way as Roald Dahl rewrote fairy stories (*Revolting Rhymes*). How can you change the ending? Can you make people act out of character and break the myth? Can you write a triumphant ending, or add humour to it? Start with "Once upon a time there was a little child." Plan to show your stories to a friend.

## COMING TO TERMS

Unfortunately, you cannot re-write the past, no matter how painful it was, no matter how hurt and wronged you still feel. You can't undo the damage. You must learn to say goodbye to the "wish" for better parents and continue with the rest of your life. Banishing the longing for what might have been will enable you to make room for what can be and the "real" people in your life, even if they are not perfect.

To help you come to terms with the past and to understand how this colours present relationships, you may decide you want counselling. Some contact addresses of counselling agencies are given at the end of the book.

## FURTHER READING

Angelou, M. (1984). *I know why the caged bird sings*. London: Virago.
Bass, E., & Thornton, L. (1983). *I never told anyone*. New York: Harper & Row.
Morris, M. (1982). *If I should die before I wake*. New York: Black Swan.
Spring, J. (1991). *Cry hard and swim. The story of an incest survivor.* London: Virago.

The four books above are written by people who have personally experienced sexual abuse.

Bain, O., & Saunders, M. (1990). *Out in the open: A guide for young people who have been sexually abused*. London: Virago Upstarts. This book was specifically written for sexually abused teenagers discussing what happens once the truth is out.

Gallagher, V. (1991). *Becoming whole again. Help for women survivors of childhood sexual abuse.* Blue Ridge Summit, PA: TAB Books.

Stones, R. (1987). *Too close encounters and what to do about them.* London: Magnet

CHAPTER TEN

# Food for Thought

We all have ideas of how the world and people in it work, even if most of the time these are unconscious. A lot of these ideas stem from childhood (i.e. if your parents always told you that you are a nice and worthwhile person, it is likely you will think of yourself as nice and worthwhile, whereas if they told you that you are fat and selfish, it is very likely you will grow up thinking you are fat and selfish). On the basis of these ideas we try to understand what goes on around us ("even though I have made a few mistakes, my friends will go on liking me because they like me for what I am" or "people won't like me unless I am perfect" or "unless I please people, they will guess how selfish I am"). We also use our ideas to predict what the likely outcome of events will be ("that nice boy who asked me out will probably never do so again as I am so stupid and ugly"). Problems arise when a person's set of ideas is not continually updated in the light of new experiences and a person gets stuck with a number of beliefs and ways of coping learnt as a child, but which are false or inappropriate. Sufferers of eating disorders usually have many self-defeating beliefs about themselves and the world at large. Often these come from difficult childhood experiences. In other cases the eating disorder itself makes the person feel that they are hopeless, disgusting, a mess, stupid, or worthless. Many of the irrational thoughts are focused on, and fuelled by, the eating symptoms (e.g. "I have binged again/ I've been unable to eat enough again, I am a truly worthless person"), others centre on life in general (e.g. "my boyfriend left me, I am so unattractive, I will never find another man again").

## TOAD IN A HOLE

Often sufferers of eating disorders have been indoctrinated from childhood to believe that they were not quite right.

*Joy*

Joy had felt low about herself for years, and as a teenager she had taken several overdoses and cut herself. She confessed that she had never felt liked and cared for as a child. She noticed that there were many photographs of her brother and sister around the house, but there were none of her. It was a family joke that she had been a very ugly baby and child. Her mother had a friend who had a daughter two months older than Joy. Throughout her life Joy had been negatively compared to the friend's daughter. She was ridiculed and humiliated because she was the ugly, chubby one. The two families spent all their time together, and Joy could never get away from being put down.

As in Joy's case, there may have been powerful family myths built up around you (not clever enough, not pretty enough, not ...). The scars of being the family's ugly duckling can last for a long time.

*Jameela*

Jameela's father was from India and her mother from Ireland. She grew up in a small village in the South East of England. "I had a lot of trouble at school. I was often teased because of my exotic looks and somehow grew up thinking that my differentness meant I was defective in some way. Even now, whenever the slightest thing goes

A TOAD IN THE HOLE

wrong, I tell myself over and over how worthless I am." This led to her avoiding social contact. Because she felt defective, she didn't know what to say or how to interact, and so she appeared unfriendly, standoffish, and aloof and was left alone.

Do any of these ring true for you?

- I don't know what to say when I'm with others, I therefore avoid social meetings of any sort.
- I lack confidence, I think that people won't like me, will criticise me, or will find me stupid.
- I fear that if I speak it will come out wrong, and people will laugh.

These self-defeating thoughts often go round continuously in a person's head, nagging and undermining, wearing a person out, intensifying if the slightest thing goes wrong. Worse still, they actually make things go wrong. Say, for example, you expect other people not to like you. You therefore behave as if they didn't like you by being withdrawn and defensive. It is, then, likely that other people will treat you as if something was wrong with you. This will strengthen your belief that people don't like you. This is what's called a self-fulfilling prophecy.

Self-defeating thoughts are the root of depression and low self-esteem, and they make eating problems worse. It is, therefore, very important to try to become aware of these thoughts/beliefs and to question them.

## THE GLOOM-AND-DOOM SCENARIO

A sense of helplessness, hopelessness, and inevitability is often the result of irrational thoughts that combine three elements: (1) you shouldering the responsibility when things go wrong ("I let her down"); (2) thinking that things will be the same forever ("I ALWAYS let her down"); and (3) things will be the same wherever you go ("I always let EVERYBODY down"—in other words, the feeling that failures are due to your own doing or personality, and that this will always be the case in all situations. This is a really paralysing attitude to have because it makes you feel you have no control over events and can't change anything or that the events over which you do have some control will inevitably turn out bad. Ultimately this leads to depression.

## ISN'T LIFE DREADFUL?

Are you one of the people for whom life is dreadful? Just one catastrophe, disaster, major flop after another? Maybe you are truly unlucky—there are some people who seem to attract problems, but if everything always seems to go wrong, especially for you, maybe it is something to do with your attitudes rather than how things really are.

*Gina*

Gina always went around thinking the worst things only happened to her. Her mother was very bitter about having been left by Gina's father when Gina was little and had always talked about how hard and unfair life was. "I suppose I somehow learnt to see things through her eyes, to always concentrate on the negative side of things. Everything was an insurmountable hurdle put in my path to trip me up. And I'd let it trip me up. In some ways I draw some weird sort of satisfaction from things being difficult for me. My husband is just the opposite—difficulties are there to be overcome."

## WRACKED BY GUILT?

A powerful sense of having done something wrong accompanies many sufferers of eating disorders in their daily life. Guilty thoughts may be especially strong after eating. "I reached the point where, even after eating a bunch of grapes, I'd feel totally guilty, like I'd committed a major crime. I'd know it's total nonsense and yet I'd have these pangs of guilt." Guilt is a hard problem to tackle.

- Try to imagine a court-room scenario, with the judge shouting out, "The accused has been found guilty of eating a bunch of grapes (or whatever it is you feel guilty of—eating 5 cream buns ... not being sympathetic to her friend's problems at all times ... not visiting her parents often enough). She will be sentenced to 5 years' hard labour."
- How might a brilliant defense lawyer tackle the accusation against you and sway the jury in your favour? He might say, "What has the accused actually done wrong? Since when is it a crime in this country to eat a bunch of grapes? I admit to eating a bunch of grapes only this

morning. Is there anyone in this courtroom who has never eaten grapes?"

## PLEASE, PLEASE THEM

Some people feel under a constant obligation to others. They have a central feeling that they will only be loved on condition that they are worthy, clever, charming, or attractive enough. Sheila MacLeod, in her book, *The Art of Starvation* (1981, London: Virago), describes this. "The anorexic is behaving like a person who has never experienced mother-love. She is behaving as if the world were full of fathers only, fathers who have to be impressed, pleased or gratified." And, of course, the same is true for many sufferers of bulimia.

### The Plastic Pleaser

*John*

John had been sensitive as a child; he was aware how distressed his mother was when he and his brothers came in dirty and made a mess in the house she took pains to keep clean. He couldn't bear her cold silences, which accompanied her anger. Homesick at boarding-school, he felt it was his duty to cope. It was difficult to steer a safe course between punishment with severe beatings from the teachers for failing to come up to standard and bullying from other boys for being a swot or goody-goody. He became highly skilled at aiming to please.

Like John,

- Do you fear not pleasing others, because you might fail to get love or approval or be criticised or abused?
- Do you please others regardless of how you feel, suppress your own feelings, try to understand how others tick so you can maintain their goodwill?
- Are you unable to say no and take on too much in order not to let others down, or put things off because you can't bear to get it wrong?
- Do you keep feelings bottled up because they signal inner needs?

- Are you concerned that you may dissolve into tears or explode into anger if you let anything out?
- Are you frightened of being ridiculed or considered as wet or a wimp?

If any of these seem true, can you think of any situations from the past that could explain things? When you recognise that you are falling into the pleasing pit, stop yourself and try to think how your behaviour is affecting others:

- If you never let people know what you really want or feel, they are left trying to read your mind and divine your wishes. Of course they will get it wrong at times, which gives them a profound sense of failure and deprives them of the pleasure of pleasing you. They may perceive you as being superior and aloof.
- If you aim to say and do everything to give in to others, they will think of you as spineless, characterless, without individuality; they are bound to find you uninteresting.
- If you always try to please, you will get angry and frustrated if your efforts are not noticed, and it is impossible not to let this show, even in subtle ways.
- Being a silent martyr can be intensely irritating, as it presumes that you are right and does not give you any opportunity to see the other person's side of things.
- Aiming to please may be a selfish wish, as it may involve taking the moral high ground, but it also deprives everyone else of the chance to give and to be nice.

## The Shrew Untamed

Some people take the opposite stand to pleasing/placation as their way of coping and refuse to meet the demands made by others: "If I must—I won't." Often these two coping styles coexist in the same person, who may be all charm and helpfulness to acquaintances and yet appear stubborn and unyielding to members of the family.

- Do you feel caged and restricted if obliged to do things?
- How does this make you feel? Furious, frightened, or defiant?
- Does this refusal mean that you can't reach your full potential?

John shifted between these two poles. Most of the time he did what others wanted, but armed with the cloak of his bulimia nervosa, he was able to make a stand and refuse to do things.

## How to Struggle out of the Pleasing Pit

Your aim with both of these two modes of coping is to strike a balance between looking after your needs—i.e. trying to ensure that things are good enough for you—and doing what will please others. Initially it may be difficult for you to establish what you want—you may need to tackle this using a formalised problem-solving approach (see chapter 2). Once you have thought of some alternative ways of behaving, you can write a balance sheet, which will help you define what seems best for you. Once you have established your goals, you may need to use assertiveness skills to claim them (see chapter 11).

Remember to chant these battle-cries to give yourself strength:

- You cannot please everyone all of the time!
- You cannot love or be loved by everyone!
- Sticking up for yourself is not selfish!

## THE DICTATORSHIP OF CONTROL

A common way in which people with eating disorders organise their thinking is to aim for total control as there is an underlying fear of chaos.

*Linda*

Linda kept the flat in which she lived in perfect order. Each evening she would spend an hour cleaning the bathroom and kitchen. Her flatmates did not see this as an indirect message for them to work hard to keep the flat clean. Rather, they saw this behaviour as boring and unpleasantly intrusive into their lives. They avoided Linda whenever possible and joked about their "little housewife" flatmate behind her back. As soon as possible they said they were leaving. At work, her need for control and order led her repeatedly to check on the people with whom she worked to ensure that they were doing what she asked. She would attempt to delegate some organisational task but would later do the job herself, sending letters that overrode the decisions made by her colleagues. Her workmates found this intolerable; they shunned her at social occasions and laughed at her once she had left the room. A further way that Linda controlled her life was to control her eating and exercise habits.

Under my thumb....

- Like Linda, do you have to clean or check on things obsessively or keep things in perfect order at all times?
- Sit and try to image in detail what you fear might happen if you fail to come up to your standards. Close your eyes, and conjure up the situation. Play through it slowly. What would you do, how could you cope? Imagine a friend of yours whom you admire as strong. How would they cope, what would they think and do? Is a critical inner voice trying to sabotage you? Tell your critic that no matter what happens you will either find a way of coping, or enlist help.
- Plan to experiment gradually by giving up one aspect of control. This might mean relaxing some control over your dietary rules. Or perhaps you will deliberately leave some housework undone, e.g. delay the washing-up by 10 minutes. Observe the anxiety and guilt that will overcome you, and see how long they last. If you survive your small experiment successfully, you may be ready to relinquish excessive control in the next area. You must practice challenging your excessive standards every day in little ways.

Here are some arguments that may come in useful when you are trying to tackle this type of thinking trap:

- I cannot control fate—life will throw up events without any justice.
- Although I can do some things to stack the dice of life in my favour, luck also plays a role.
- Learning to tolerate a bit of mess and chaos is an important survival skill.

## The Ace of Asceticism

Another way in which the craving for control may show itself is to restrict our own instinctive drives. This may lead to the feeling that it is wrong to have our own wishes or needs met. If we do acknowledge our need for comfort, we feel guilty or lacking in moral fibre. If we do get what we want, we are sickened by our selfishness or childishness.

### Victoria

Victoria was the youngest daughter of a Kenyan businessman. Her father was very successful, which meant that he and her mother were busy and often out in the evenings for business reasons. It always seemed an imposition to Victoria to ask for help with homework or to chat about school. Victoria felt her parents were too busy to be interested in her; she had to cope. She felt very different and isolated from the other girls at school, as she was the only African in her class. She had no want for material things. Her father bought her a flat when she was 15 and arranged for this to be rented out. From the age of 15 onwards, her father's business concerns took him and his wife back to Kenya for five months every year. Victoria was left in the charge of her sister, who was one year older but who had a close relationship with a boyfriend. She came to us with an eating disorder, crying for no reason, and with a pervasive sense of loneliness.

- Like Victoria, you may describe your parents in glowing terms as they may have provided you with every material comfort, but they may have neglected your emotional development and the need to give sufficient time, support, and attention to you.
- Like Victoria, you may feel it is ridiculous to feel like a deprived baby with distress that you cannot define when your parents treat you as an adult. Somehow, however, the silver spoon jars against your teeth.
- Your parents may do the opposite and make you run short materially to "strengthen you". You then feel furious but can't explain or admit it when they pay more for vet's fees for the cat, than they do on helping you start at university.
- Alternatively, the neediness inside may drive you to use or fantasise about other forms of comfort—eating, taking drugs, spending money, or sexual relationships. Because you do not understand what underlies this need for comfort and care, it seems like greed.

## The Patina of Power

The same underlying mechanisms can lead to the drive to create superwoman who can be best and tackle anything. The compulsive perfectionist strives for bigger and better without reflecting on the need or the appropriateness of the goal. Trying to give your best, if you can, is not a bad thing and will be helpful to you in many walks of life. However, people with eating problems often have unrealistically high expectations of themselves and the world—they don't just try to do their best, they have to succeed at being best at all times; everything has got to be flawless and just so. This can include their personal appearance, their work, and their interpersonal relationships.

Ask yourself the following questions: Why do you need such success? Why have you got to outsmart or outshine others? Why do you need to compete so hard?

Maybe your drive for perfectionism is the result of an underlying fear that nobody will like you unless you are superwoman and that errors, mistakes, sloppiness, oversights, and carelessness are unforgivable. Or you may be frightened of chaos, or are lonely and lost without a goal. Often a less-than-perfect performance makes the person think that they are totally useless, but boy, how exhausting it is trying to be perfect! Not just that—perfectionism strangles the messy, lively, spontaneous, creative side of your personality.

Society's approval of your striving for financial security or to be the best at your job may lull you into the belief that you do not have to question why you are so needy.

### Emily

Emily became Personal Assistant to the Political Editor of a National Newspaper. "It was an incredibly ambitious, high-powered work environment." Emily did several hours' unpaid overtime every day to prove to her boss that she was excellent. "I tried to read his mind and do things he might ask me to do before he even asked. I wanted him to think that I was the best Personal Assistant he had ever had." However, she rarely got any praise, and one day she overheard her boss talking about her to someone else: "Oh yes Emily, my new P.A., she's trying awfully hard; her work is okay, but she's so tense, it rubs off on everyone else in the office." Emily was shattered. You can see that Emily's attempts to be perfect were fuelled by her need to please.

## OVER TO YOU

Each time you feel inappropriately upset or act against your own interest, look for your thinking errors—thoughts that fuel your upset. One way to establish whether a belief is rational or irrational is to ask yourself the following questions:

- What and where is the evidence for that?
- What other explanations are there?
- What would you think about this belief if you were another person looking at yourself?
- Am I trying to please, to be perfect or be in control?

You need to identify the patterns of behaving, which serve you badly. It can be pretty difficult to "catch" your self-defeating thoughts in action, as they come on so quickly and automatically. You may find that your self-defeating thoughts come from one or several of the areas outlined above, or they may not fit neatly into any of the categories at all.

When you have recognised some of the thinking traps in your own life, start trying to notice them each time they happen and record them in your diary.

- In your diary, write down the "A's" (antecedents)—thoughts or feelings that happened just before you felt emotionally disturbed or behaved self-defeatingly—and find the "C's" (consequences)—disturbed feelings or self-defeating behaviour that resulted.

- Make two columns: In the first, put your self-defeating irrational belief, e.g."I must do well or I am totally useless." In the second, put a rational thought, e.g. "I'd prefer to do well but don't have to."

Table 10.1 lists examples of the irrational thoughts experienced by Emily, whom we introduced to you earlier, and the more rational thoughts she learnt to replace them with in treatment.

- To add to this method of challenging your self-defeating thoughts, it is useful to have strategies in which you change the consequences of these thoughts, not just by replacing them with more appropriate thoughts, but by what you do. Have a plan of action well thought out, so that you can use it the next time one of these self-defeating patterns emerges. For example, phone a friend, go and visit someone, go through the balance sheet, etc.

Below are some more of the argued responses to the different self-defeating thoughts shared by sufferers of eating disorders. Some are to do with eating, some are to do with other areas of life.

*Eva:* "It is irrational for me to be overwhelmed by guilt for having slightly more food than I think is right."

"I find it difficult to eat normally, but that doesn't mean it's impossible."

"When people refuse my invitations, it doesn't mean that I have done something wrong."

"Doing something foolish makes me a person who acts foolishly, not a total fool."

*Jane:* "I feel very good if I can keep my weight down. That doesn't prove that it is good for me to do this."

*Val:* "Even when I have a strong urge to eat, I don't have to."

*Alison:* "It is not awful to be disapproved of, only uncomfortable. I can always choose to accept myself, even when I do stupid acts."

TABLE 10.1
Emily's Self-defeating Thoughts and Counter-arguments

| Irrational Thoughts | Rational Thoughts |
|---|---|
| If I am not outstanding in my work, people will see me as a totally insignificant person, who isn't worthwhile knowing. | That doesn't follow at all. There is much more of significance in a person than their performance at work. And besides, even if I am not outstanding, I can still do competent work. |
| To be worthwhile as a human being, I must be loved and approved of by everyone. | You can't rate a person by who loves or hates them. |

"When I make a mistake, such as eating more than I feel I should, or get something wrong, this only proves that I am fallible and human."
*Chantal:* "With hard work, I am sure I can manage to eat more over the next few days. It will be great not to feel exhausted."
"Not knowing how this (important) project will turn out makes me anxious and concerned, but perhaps I can also use it to be a bit more curious and adventurous about things."
*Tracey:* "Falling back several times and losing weight is a challenge that may enable me to learn how to accept myself fully with all my fallibility and foolish behaviour."
"Having lost several jobs in a row may provide me with the challenge and determination to find and keep a suitable job."

## SHAKE OFF SHAME

Feelings of shame, embarrassment, and humiliation are closely linked to the idea that you must be perfect or else nobody will like you. To beat these feelings, try to think of something you can do that you consider would be shameful, foolish, or ridiculous and that you would be particularly ashamed to do in public—not something like walking in the street naked, which would get you into real trouble, and not an act like slapping someone, which would hurt or bother other people—something you would really like to do but wouldn't have done or something merely foolish that you would not normally do. Think vividly of doing this act, and let yourself feel ashamed about it.

Go and do your "shameful act" in public, and while doing it work on your feelings so that you don't feel ashamed and embarrassed and humiliated, even though others may be laughing at you and thinking you're a fool for doing it. Plan to perform at least one "shameful" act each week. These are some ideas other patients have given:

• Wear an out-of-fashion suit or dress that is still serviceable.
• Don't wear any make-up, and go around with holes in your tights for a day.
• Dress comfortably for a formal affair.
• Tell a friend or relative about your eating disorder.
• Confess your inadequacies to significant people.
• Stuff balloons or cushions under your clothes, so that you seem to be much fatter than you are. Go around like this for a day.
• Go into the public changing room in a shop or a swimming bath, rather than into a single cubicle.
• Go to a joke shop or to a theatrical outfitters, and get something that will make you look as though your stomach or bottom is very big.
• Deliberately let a small thing go wrong at work.

# FURTHER READING

Beck, A.T. (1976). *Cognitive therapy and the emotional disorder.* London: Penguin Books.

Blackburn, I.M. (1987). *Coping with depression.* Edinburgh: Chambers.

Burns, D, D. (1990). *The feeling good handbook.* New York: Penguin Group, USA (Plume).

Carter-Scott, C. (1988). *Negaholics. Overcome your lack of confidence. A twelve-step programme to recovery.* London: Century.

Palladino, C. D. (1989). *Developing self-esteem. A positive guide for personal success.* London: Kogan Page Ltd.

Wilde-McCormick, E. (1990). *Change for the better. A life-changing self-help psychotherapy programme.* London: Unwin Paperbacks.

# CHAPTER ELEVEN

# Finding Your Voice

Did you recognise yourself in the plastic pleaser or the subject of control or standards as described in chapter 10? Are you a person whose life is ruled and ruined by shoulds, drained by giving and giving and giving, until you feel totally tired out?

Do others take advantage of you because you will say "yes" to whatever they ask you, even if you would like to shout "no, no, no"? Are you unable to refuse any favours for fear of hurting the feelings of the other person irrevocably and beyond repair? Do you worry that, if you ever say what you want, you might be seen as totally self-obsessed and selfish?

If your answer is "yes" to any of these questions, read on. You suffer from lack of assertiveness! This is often the result of having extremely low self-esteem, feeling that you are totally insignificant or unloveable.

*Sally*

Sally is a case in point. She is a 20-year-old secretary in a small, successful company. "I feel nobody is really interested in me, I am not a very nice or interesting person to be with." When Sally came into treatment, she felt so bad about herself that she constantly had to pacify her feelings of guilt, shame, or self-disgust and prove her worth and usefulness by being everything to everybody, looking after others practically or emotionally. "We are four girls in the office. If our boss pops round the corner and says, "who is going to make us a cup of coffee, then?" it's always me who jumps up.

Needless to say, the washing-up is also left to me. The others just won't do it. I often stay behind to clear up when everybody has gone home." Sally also regularly took on twice as much work as everybody else. Once or twice her boss tried to be supportive to her by asking one of the other girls in the office to take some of Sally's load. "I didn't like that at all; I know he was only trying to be helpful, but I felt totally guilty afterwards." Is Sally a masochist or a martyr? Probably neither. However, she had got very used to letting herself be used as a doormat and found it very threatening not to be one. She feared that, if she gave up the role of a doormat, others would reject her.

Sometimes the fear of a lot of pent-up anger or frustration coming out is what stops a person from speaking their mind.

*Cindy*

Cindy, a 20-year-old student, shared a flat with another girl. "Although we are supposed to be equals in the flat, I don't seem to have the right to say what I think about things. Alison, my flatmate, is very outspoken and often really thoughtless. It's been irritating me for a while. The other day she said in front of a group of people whom she had invited for her birthday dinner that she would not pay for a meal for me, as I would sick it up anyway. I was furious. I would have liked to kick or punch her or shout at her. Instead, I said nothing and just gave her a nervous little smile."

## LEARNING TO STAND YOUR GROUND

We can communicate our wants/needs/feelings in three different ways:

1. *Passive*
   Where your own wants/needs/feelings are silenced. This kind of communication may be given with a slumped body, downcast eyes, and a hesitant, giggly, or whining voice. It uses: "maybe", "I wonder if you could, only, just", "It's all right, don't bother".
2. *Assertive*
   Where you express your own wants, needs, and feelings, but also take into account the feelings of the person to whom you are talking.
3. *Aggressive*
   Where you only consider your own wants, needs, and feelings. Inappropriate anger or hostility is loudly or explosively uttered. There is use of threats: "you'd better", or put-downs: "come on, you must be kidding", or evaluative comments: "should", "I thought you would know better".

We all deal with different situations in these three ways. Women with eating difficulties often swing between the passive and aggressive poles and find it difficult to get onto a middle ground.

Think of the last time you behaved passively, suppressing your own feelings. Reconstruct the behaviour chain of this event (see chapter 2).

A. *Where, What, With Whom, and When?*
- What were your thoughts?
- What were the feelings (that you chose to suppress)?
- The thoughts that commonly lead to this pattern are:
  - "If I say something he/she won't like me"
  - "It's silly for me to be upset"
B. *Passive Behaviour*
- How, in what way, did you let someone walk over you?
C. *What Were the Positive and Negative Consequences of this?*

Assertive rather than passive behaviour is a skill you will need to learn and use as a way of finding the middle ground.

## ANYTHING FOR A QUIET LIFE?

"Why should I learn to be assertive? Isn't it terribly risky?" you may ask. Whatever your reasons for not voicing your own needs, wants, and feelings, whilst in the short term it may seem easiest, in the long term it can seriously damage your physical and mental health.

- Not being assertive leads to a gradual build-up of frustration, which will keep your bulimia going and can also lead to other health problems like headaches and backaches.
- Others may sympathise with the poor downtrodden you and may seem to "like" your non-assertiveness. However, they'll soon become irritated by you, especially if you moan about how unfair life is or look so unwell with your bulimia and yet don't do anything about it.
- Ignoring conflict might make it go away in the short term, but in the long term tension and frustration increase. It is far healthier to deal with situations as they arise.

You may still say, "This all sounds like a lot of effort to me, and it carries the risk of alienating people around me. I am too frightened even to try." Nobody is saying you should change overnight to being assertive at all times in all situations, but you should at least have the choice as to whether or not you want to behave assertively in specific circumstances.

## GROUND-RULES FOR ASSERTIVE BEHAVIOUR

Like everyone else, you have basic human rights: the right to hold and express your own opinions; the right to make mistakes; the right to refuse requests without guilt; the right to change your mind; the right to set your own priorities and goals; and the right to judge your own behaviour, thoughts, and emotions and to take responsibility for the consequences.

- Think ahead—before negotiating, be absolutely clear what you want to achieve and what your rights (and those of other people) are. Anticipate any possible objections, and work out your responses— being prepared will boost your confidence.
- Choose your timing if you can. Asking your boss for a pay rise as she pushes past your desk on the way to a meeting is not the right way to tackle it! Make an appointment with her to discuss the matter privately.
- When you make a request, be specific and direct. Avoid unassertive words like "only", "rather", and "maybe". Don't say, "I wondered whether maybe I could be put forward for promotion." Say, "Could I be put forward for promotion?"
- Criticise behaviour, not the person. Stick to facts and not judgements. Avoid words like "always", "never", and "impossible". Say something positive about the person or situation. After you have said what you had to say, don't hover. Don't undo what you said by apologising.
- When you have to say no, suggest alternatives. "I am afraid I can't help do the baby-sitting for you tonight, but I am free tomorrow if that's any help."
- Use the "broken record" technique on people who try to change the subject or convince you to reverse a decision. Repeat your point calmly, no matter what the other person says.
- Make eye contact. Adopt an upright and relaxed posture—shoulders down and arms by your side, not crossed defensively.

There are other techniques if you are being baited by criticism.

- Calmly accept that there may be some truth in what your critic says, but remain your own judge of what you do.
- Negative assertion: accept your errors or faults without having to apologise.
- Prompt criticism in order to use the information if it is helpful or to exhaust it if it is manipulative.

## HOW TO PUT ASSERTIVENESS INTO PRACTICE

You will probably have seen some of the things outlined above in other books or in women's magazines, but you may still be wondering how to put it all into practice.

For situations where you can plan beforehand:

- Practice what you want to say in front of the mirror.
- Make a tape-recording of what you want to say.
- Role-play the situation with a friend, change roles, take on the person to whom you make the request.

There are, of course, situations where you have to think on your feet. You may have got so used to saying "yes" to other people's requests that you only notice after you have said "yes" that you really didn't want to take on the extra commitment. Remember, you have a right to change your mind. Ring up the person to whom you said "yes" and say, "I am sorry, but I will not be able to do the extra job after all."

You may also find it difficult to come up with an assertive response when someone puts you on the spot. You don't have to. You can tell the person later how you felt about what they said. Say, "I want to talk to you about what you said yesterday. It really hurt me when you said ..."

The first time you assert yourself will be terrifying, but you will improve with practice. You will find that behaving assertively leads to increased self-confidence, and that, in turn, will lead to more assertive behaviour. Gradually your life will become more balanced.

Below we give an example of a tricky situation one of our patients struggled with.

*Ursula*

Ursula is a well-liked, gentle sort of person, who in her spare time plays in an orchestra. One of the other players, a girl called Lynne, desperately tried to befriend Ursula. Lynne would ring Ursula up daily to tell her for hours about all the problems in her life, but she never seemed keen to listen to Ursula. She would repeatedly ask Ursula to go out with her in a way that was difficult to refuse: "You are not doing anything tonight. That's great. I have got two theatre tickets, would you like to go with me, I will pick you up in the car." Ursula felt overwhelmed at first but then got intensely irritated with Lynne. She avoided her as much as possible. She instructed her parents to tell Lynne she wasn't in when she rang. She thought of not going to the orchestra any more, although she enjoyed it very much. Part of her also felt sorry for Lynne, who seemed to have few other friends. She thought if she refused any of Lynne's approaches, she would hurt her and felt that, by accepting theatre tickets and other small favours, she had lost her right to assert herself and set limits in the relationship. It was obvious that something needed to be done. It was probable that, through partially avoiding Lynne, Ursula fuelled her persistence and that the only way to make herself freer again was to stand up to Lynne. This is how Ursula eventually asserted herself, by using the "broken record" technique:

*Telephone Conversation*

*Ursula:* "Hello, Ursula here."

*Lynne* (slightly reproachfully): "Hi, I've been trying to get hold of you all day, where have you been?"

*Ursula* (somewhat defensively): "Well, I had to go out and do a few things."

*Lynne:* "Are you in tonight?"

*Ursula:* "Yes, I am."

*Lynne:* "Are you doing anything specific?"

*Ursula:* "No nothing really, just watching TV."

*Lynne* (sounding enthusiastic): "Oh good, I thought I might just come over and see you. I'll pick up a pizza on the way. Would 8.00 p.m. be okay?"

*Ursula:* "Actually, I don't think I feel up to seeing anybody tonight. I just need some time to myself."

*Lynne* (somewhat surprised): "Oh, don't be such a bore. All that sitting around on your own does you no good whatsoever.

*Ursula:* "I am sorry you feel I am a bore, but I really don't feel up to seeing you tonight. Perhaps we could meet at the week-end."

*Lynne* (seductively): "I just thought it would be nice to meet tonight; there are a few new developments with Alan that I want to tell you about."

*Ursula:* "I'd love to hear about it, but I am just really not up to it tonight."

*Lynne* (more and more upset): "I don't understand what's going on. You are telling me you are doing nothing, and yet I can't come round. I think that's really selfish of you. You don't do that to an old friend."

*Ursula:* "I am sorry, but I really want to be on my own tonight."

It was obvious that as the telephone conversation progressed, Lynne was trying to make Ursula feel very uncomfortable and guilty. Ursula coped well by not rising to the bait and by not getting into an argument about whether or not she was acting selfishly.

# FURTHER READING

Butler, P.E. (1982). *Self-assertion for women*. New York: Harper and Row.

Dickson. A. (1985). *A Woman in your own right. Assertiveness and you*. London: Quartet Books.

Hare, B. (1988). *Be assertive*. London: Macdonald Optima

CHAPTER TWELVE

# The Seduction of Self-destruction

Alcohol and drug abuse, shoplifting and overspending are common in people with eating disorders. Underlying these problems are many different emotional reasons that parallel those covered in chapter 10 as underlying your binge eating. At times these patterns of behaviour are used as an escape route from the unpleasant effects of the eating disorder, numbing the feelings of guilt over bingeing or counteracting pangs of hunger. Or they may constitute a remedy to some other problem—for example, an inability to sleep or to relax is treated with alcohol or drugs. Alternatively, they are used in an attempt to "cure" some unpleasant state of mind, like boredom, depression, or anxiety. From rather innocent casual beginnings, enduring self-destructive patterns can emerge, as you will see from the cases described in this chapter.

## THE SLIPPERY SLOPE OF BOOZE AND DRUGS

Strong social anxieties commonly lead to drinking/taking drugs. Especially if you "feel fat", you may find it difficult to go out unless you have drunk something.

*Bridget*
"I have always been a very shy person. Especially when I fancy someone, I get totally tongue-tied and clam up. I start pouring with sweat, and I can't think of anything to say. Other people must think I am totally boring when I am like that. My bulimia has made it

even more difficult to be relaxed with other people. The only way I can go out and have a good time is if I had something to drink. I usually have half a bottle of wine before I go out. Then I'll carry on drinking all night. I often can't really remember very much the next day, but others have told me that I behave totally outrageously when I am like that."

Of course, if you are always drunk or drugged when out, others will notice and will come to see you in an unfavourable light, which is what happened to Bridget.

"Some good friends have said to me that when I am drunk I am not very pleasant to be with. I stagger about, I make jokes that only I find funny, and I am very provocative with men. On one or two occasions I have actually got into bed with people whom I had never met and whom I would never want to see again when I am sober."

Sometimes drink/drugs are the result of the "I can't stand it, life is too awful" syndrome. Drink is used to ease the pain of living, as the examples of Julie and Moira show. But, of course, once a pattern has been established where your whole life revolves around drink/drugs, life is likely to remain awful and get worse.

## Julie

Julie had been a promising dancer, but she had been thrown out of dance school because of her bulimia. "All my hopes were crushed. I hadn't learnt a thing. Frankly, I didn't want to do anything else. I had spent years dancing, thinking about being a dancer. I was so angry—angry with the school for throwing me out, angry with myself that I hadn't hidden my bulimia better from them, angry with my parents, with the whole world. Then I met Kevin, and we started a relationship. Kevin likes his drink, and soon we were out in the pub night after night. Neither of us had a job. My mum didn't like him, but I didn't care. I just drank and drank and drank, night after night. I couldn't stop. At some stage I tried to leave Kevin. He wouldn't let me. He got very angry and beat me up."

## Moira

"I smoke dope every day. What am I like without it? Tense, anxious, eating myself up with worry about trivial things. I am the sort of person who will always find something to be worried about. I go over things endlessly in my mind—how I behaved in certain situations, what I should and shouldn't have said in certain conversations. Dope just blocks all of that out. Sometimes I worry about it, it really saps your energy levels, I have no drive, no motivation."

Some drugs, like amphetamines, help one lose weight, but the price to be paid is high: "When I was on amphetamines, I was so hyped up I could never sleep. My personality changed, and I became very suspicious." Many drugs available from private slimming clinics are of this type. These drugs are not prescribed in the NHS as it is realised that their side-effects far outweigh any value that they have.

### Ecstasy

There has been a lot of publicity about Ecstasy, and this drug has been promoted as a designer drug with no untoward consequences. This is by no means true. A recent article by Henry, Jeffreys, and Dawling in the *Lancet* (1992, Vol. 340, pp. 384–387) reviews all the medical consequences, which range from liver failure to sudden death.

### Caffeine and Artificial Sweeteners

Stop! Don't skip over this bit just because you are not taking any street drugs. What about your smoking? What about your caffeine and artificial sweetener consumption? We often forget what a powerful "drug" caffeine is. It can lead to anxiety, panic, and tremors. In excess, your sleep and thoughts get disturbed. It may become difficult to put your thoughts together; you may get suspicious of others. You should ask yourself the same questions as those outlined in the section on alcohol below, replacing the word "alcohol" with the particular "drug" you take. Again, if you answer more than three questions with "yes', you are probably heading towards being dependent on the drugs you are taking.

## SHOULD I BE WORRIED ABOUT MY ALCOHOL INTAKE?

If you have an eating disorder, you run a much greater risk of becoming addicted to alcohol and drugs, for a number of reasons. Research has consistently found that problems with alcohol and drugs are much more common amongst families of women with eating disorders. We do not know exactly what causes the same type of problem to run through the generations. What is passed on may be some genetic vulnerability, or it may be that if drinking a lot is a way of responding to problems in your family, you grow up picking up the same way of behaving. There are also important physical reasons—your restriction of food—which make you vulnerable to the seductive powers of alcohol. Your body will quickly learn that this is the only source of calories you will allow yourself. This exaggerates the craving for alcohol.

Alcoholic drinks have "empty" calories; they contain none of the additional substances such as minerals and vitamins that are required for health. Moreover, the body's methods of detoxifying alcohol use up the vitamin reserves of the body. You therefore run an increased risk of vitamin deficiency if you drink alcohol. These deficiencies lead to brain damage—your memory is particularly at risk.

## What Are the Safe Limits?

To calculate your weekly intake, it is best to count up the units you drink:

1 unit of alcohol = half a pint of beer
= a single measure of spirits
= a glass of wine
= a small glass of sherry
= a measure of vermouth or aperitif

Drinks poured at home are usually much more generous than pub or restaurant measures. So, in calculating your units, you need to take this into account. Write down your daily intake in your diary for a week.

You may have read that for women up to 14 units a week, spread throughout the week, carries no long-term health risks (for men up to 21 units). However, for the reasons described above, we cannot be sure what level is safe for women with eating disorders with their precarious state of nutrient balance. If you concentrate your drinking into, say, two bouts and get drunk, you're increasing the risks to yourself even without an eating disorder. If you drink more than 22 units per week (for men more than 36), damage to your health is likely. Your liver and stomach can both be affected. Your concentration may be poor, and all sorts of personal and social problems may be building up. There may be financial and legal problems, problems at work and home, and sexual difficulties, too.

Answer the following questions as honestly as possible[1]:

- Do you often drink too much? Do you often think you should cut down?
- Does alcohol cause problems for you and make you feel guilty?
- Has anyone ever objected to your drinking or criticised you about it?
- Have you ever had a drink in the morning to steady your nerves or to get rid of a hangover?

If the answer to one or several of these questions is YES, go on.

- Do you often find that, when you start drinking, you end up drinking more than you were planning to?
- Do you often try to cut down or stop drinking alcohol?
- Do you spend a lot of time drinking, being high, or being hung over?

- Do you ever drink while doing something where it might be dangerous to drink at all (like driving)?
- Do you drink so often that you start to drink instead of working or spending time at hobbies or with your family or friends?
- Does your drinking cause problems with other people?
- Does your drinking cause you significant psychological or physical problems?
- Do you find you need to drink a lot more in order to get high than you did when you first started to drink?
- Do you ever have the shakes when you cut down drinking?

If you answered more than three questions with a definite YES, you are heading towards being dependent on alcohol. As long as you are on alcohol, it will be extremely difficult to make progress with your eating disorder. You may want to contact Alcohol Concern to see what services are available (the address is given at the end of the book).

## Have the Guts to Stop or Cut Down Your Alcohol Consumption

If you decided from what you read above that you have problems with alcohol, you should cut down drinking or even avoid alcohol altogether. Not drinking is something that is becoming much more socially acceptable. Think of the parallel case of smoking. Five or ten years ago, people who objected to others smoking in their presence were seen as weird, silly, or wet, and if they complained, they had to endure sarcastic comments and abuse. Nowadays, with increased knowledge about the health risks of active and passive smoking, it is the smokers who are at the receiving end of the criticism. This point was reached by public campaigns, but also because many people in their private lives stood up to the tyrannical behaviour of smokers.

Can you show some personal bravery if others bully you into drinking? "Oh come on, don't be a spoil-sport, why don't you just have a tiny drink?" It can be very difficult to resist someone who is determined to get you to drink. But if your friends only accept you if you drink with them, and in large amounts, are they really worth your while?

### How to Cut Down

- Take small sips only. Count the number of sips it takes to finish a glass, and then try increasing the number for the next glass, and so on.
- Do something else enjoyable while drinking that will help distract attention from the glass—for example, listening to music, talking, doing a cross-word puzzle, and so on.

- Instead of drinking your customary, favourite type of drink, change to something new. Changing the type of drink can help break old habits and reduce the amount drunk.
- Drink more slowly, and concentrate on the flavour.
- Copy a slow drinker. Identify someone who drinks slowly and shadow them, not picking up the glass until they do.
- Put the glass down after each sip. If you hold the glass, you will drink more often. Do something else with your hand instead of lifting the glass to the lips.
- Top up spirits with non-alcoholic drinks.
- As much as you can, buy your own drinks. If you have to go along with sharing rounds, do not buy yourself a drink when it is your round, or order a non-alcoholic drink.
- Take days of rest, when you don't drink alcohol, at least one day per week, or preferably two, three, or even four days per week. Take up other forms of entertainment or relaxation.
- Start drinking later than usual. For example, go to the pub later.
- Learn to refuse drinks. Role-play ways of saying no to drinks. Perhaps this is the most important assertiveness skill you need to learn. Say, for example, "No thanks, I'm cutting down", or "I am not drinking tonight, I've got a bad stomach".

Remember also, alcohol removes inhibition and therefore increases the likelihood of binges.

## DO YOU LIKE RUSSIAN ROULETTE?

Although the risk of being shot whilst shoplifting is low, the sobering fact is that most people get caught at some point. So why do so many bright and otherwise law-abiding people with eating disorders take what is a considerable risk of public humiliation, court appearance, a criminal record, and, in some cases, even being sent to prison?

There is a multitude of reasons: Some steal food when they have a strong urge to binge, or have run out of money to buy binge food. Others take things, like items of clothing or other items, that they don't need or like. Often they can't explain why they do it. The exact cause for this seemingly irrational behaviour is not understood. It has been thought that being starved has something to do with it. For example, it is known that animals who are starved hoard things. In a famous starvation experiment carried out in the 1950s in the United States, the men who participated (who were deliberately starved) began to collect and hoard all sorts of objects.

Repeated shoplifting can also be a way of dealing with boredom and depression by creating a thrill. This sense of excitement can be addictive and can lead to more and more risktaking.

*Louise*
"I have shop-lifted regularly over the last five years. It's got a lot worse since my bulimia started. As a child I was very unhappy, and I sometimes stole sweets. Now it's mainly make-up or earrings. I tend to do it when I am in one of my bingeing phases. I don't tend to do it when I am dieting and feel in control. It gives me a kick, it's exciting and terrifying."

Over time, you may get more and more hooked on it and convinced that you are not going to be caught, but, of course, most people do eventually get caught.

*Claire*
Claire began to steal things from shops a few years after her bulimia had begun. She would take clothes, food, cosmetics, and magazines. She kept long and detailed lists of everything she had stolen. "I still don't know why I did it. I just had to do it. It was like an obsession. It made me feel I was in control. I knew I was taking lots of risks, I even went into shops where they had automatic cameras installed. Maybe subconsciously I was waiting to be caught." Claire did get caught after a couple of years of regular stealing. She made no attempt to hide what she had done; the police found the lists of items she had stolen, and she had to serve a prison sentence of several months. "Prison wasn't the worst thing. What was much worse was that the whole thing was published in the local press, with my name and address. Until then I hadn't told anyone about my bulimia, and to have that dragged out was the most awful thing."

## IF I WERE A RICH MAN ...

Overspending is another self-destructive way of dealing with depression, emptiness, and boredom. Although it doesn't usually get people into legal trouble, it causes problems of its own. Many bulimic women get into such hopeless financial situations with their compulsive spending that they owe thousands of pounds to various creditors. Once you see no chance of paying your debts off, you may think you might as well carry on and, thereby, get deeper and deeper into trouble.

*Sharon*
Sharon is a single mother on social security: "I have been feeling very fed up and down lately, nothing gives me pleasure, nothing interests me. Then I suddenly got this catalogue in and began to order various things, including a hoover, a mixer, some other bits

and pieces for the kitchen. For a little while it made me feel better, like I had achieved something. That didn't last very long, though. Altogether it came up to £500. When it arrived, I didn't even open the boxes to check the contents. The stuff's been sitting in my cupboard for three weeks now, completely untouched.

Often the trap of overspending stops a person from getting on with what they'd like to do, like going on holidays, moving house, doing a college course, and so on.

*Lisa*

Lisa, a typist, lives with her parents. She owes the bank £2,000 and another £1,500 to her parents. "I can't really afford to buy anything at the moment. It'll be ages before I have paid everything off. I'd love to move out of home but I can't. There is no way I could afford to pay rent, given my current financial situation. Most of my money goes on clothes—clothes that I often don't wear, not even once. It's as if I am desperately trying to find the right thing."

## Do You Overspend or Steal?

- What is your pattern?
- Note down in your diary (Chapter 2—the ABC technique) the circumstances of overspending/stealing.
  - How do you feel at the time?
  - How do you feel afterwards?
  - What would happen if you stopped?
  - Is it that you don't allow yourself any other rewards, pleasures, or excitement?
  - Can you find other exciting or simply nice things to do?
- If your problem is shop-lifting, some people find it helpful to imagine the worst thing they can possibly think of in order to prevent themselves from doing something like stealing. In Claire's case, a nightmare scenario really did come true. Write down your own personal nightmare scenario, and try to imagine it every time you have the urge to steal something.
- If your problem is overspending, you must make a start with paying off your debts, no matter how slowly you go. It does not help to hide all the demands for payment at the back of the drawer, even though this is a common way women with eating disorders try to cope. A bank manager is used to dealing with this problem and will be able to come up with practical solutions. Is there any friend or family member in whom you can confide about this problem? Can you get them to help you by looking after your cheque book or credit cards? Can they help you budget?

## NOTE

1.  Adapted from Spitzer, R.L., Williams, J.B.W., Gibbon, M., & First, M.B. (1989). *Structured Clinical Interview for DSM-III-R: Non-patient Edition.* (SCIO, 9/1/89 Revision). New York: New York State Psychiatric Institute, Biometrics Research Department.

## FURTHER READING

Curran, V., & Golombok, S. (1985). *Bottling it up.* London: Faber and Faber.

Chick, J., & Chick, J. (1984). *Drinking problems: Information and advice for the individual, family and friends.* Edinburgh: Churchill Livingstone.

Miller, W.R., & Munoz, R.F. (1983). *How to control your drinking.* London: Sheldon Press.

Tyrer, P. (1986). *How to stop taking tranquillisers.* London: Sheldon Press.

# CHAPTER THIRTEEN

# The Web of Life: Parents, Partners, Children, and Friends

## HOME, SWEET HOME

Especially if you are still living at home, your eating disorder may cause a lot of upset in your family. Your parents may get angry with you for raiding the cupboards or for rejecting their meals. They may feel guilty and blame themselves for your eating disorder. They may alternate between trying to help by cooking for you and buying you special diet foods and angrily telling you to "snap out" of your "silly" eating problem.

You may feel that they don't understand you, that they treat you like a child, that they are getting at you, or you may be upset about the upset you cause them. It is difficult living with other people when you suffer from an eating disorder, but it is equally difficult living with someone who has an eating disorder.

*Elizabeth*

Elizabeth had had bulimia nervosa for several years. Her parents knew about this, especially her mother, who had read any book on the topic of eating disorders that she could lay her hands on. After a period of living away from home, Elizabeth moved back home because of financial difficulties. "My mother was observing me incredibly carefully. Yet she would never mention my eating disorder. She was just treating me with kid gloves. I found out from my boyfriend that she had talked to him behind my back, telling him that if he had any problem with me he could always come to her. When he told me this, I was very cross. Am I some sort of invalid? Too fragile to be talked to? I think that my mother is quite ashamed about my problem, that's why she can't talk about it directly."

## How to Improve Your Relationship with Your Parents

- If you haven't told your parents about your eating problem, think hard about whether you should. What are the gains and losses? Often parents have an inkling that something is wrong with your eating anyway, and to tell them can be a huge relief to them and to you.
- If you have told them about your eating problem and somehow this has not made matters better, they may need more information about eating disorders to be able to understand and help you. Could you give your parents this book to read? Could you suggest to them to attend a Parents' Group of the Eating Disorder Association (see address at the end of the book)?
- Spell out to your parents how they can help you. Be specific and direct. Positive suggestions work better than negative ones. So don't say, "You don't understand me, you are getting it all wrong." Say, "It would help me if I could eat with you in the evenings. Eating one meal a day with other people would be a huge step forward for me."
- Remember, your parents are only human; they are bound to get it wrong at times, just like you are. Don't expect them only to ask you about your eating problem when you feel you want to be asked. They can't read your mind.
- If things are very bad, maybe you should consider moving out. What you shouldn't do is feel upset about living at home and not do anything about it.

*Briony*

Briony, an 18-year-old student, was the youngest of a family of four. Her father was a vicar. She had been the favourite of her parents as she did very well at school and was a gifted piano player. When she developed anorexia nervosa at the age of 16 and nearly died, her parents felt awful—as if they, personally, were to blame. However, they found it even more impossible to understand or tolerate Briony's bulimic symptoms, which she developed after her anorexia. Her raiding the larder at night was seen by her family as a sign of greed and moral wickedness. "My mother and I had a shouting match every day. We had always been a very quiet, harmonious family, where people tried to talk to sort out problems."

Briony realised that her eating problem was destroying her relationship with her parents. She moved into a small flat of her own. "Once I was there, the communication between me and my parents began gradually to get better. My father actually helped me to decorate my flat. My mother agreed to go shopping with me once a week, as I had lost any idea of how much I would need. Gradually our wounds are beginning to heal. I go to see my parents every Sunday. I still feel very sad when I return to my empty flat on Sunday night, yet I think there would not have been any other solution for us."

Write a balance sheet on the pros and cons of living at home.

• If, on balance, you feel you should move out, think through carefully what the alternatives could be. Living totally alone in a bedsit in an area where you don't know anybody can make matters worse. Could you find a friend to share?

## FRIENDS

Sheila MacLeod, in her book *The Art of Starvation*, said, "the anorexic has a fundamental mistrust of personal relationships which have so often proved to be symbolic and destructive .... on the other hand she has a longing for a good relationship with another person who will understand and accept her for what she feels herself to be." Your eating disorder may make it very difficult for you to trust anybody, especially if you have been let down before. You may find it difficult to be a reliable and dependable friend yourself. You may drop out of arrangements you have made with friends because food is involved. You may drop out of going for meals or parties because you find it too frightening. Perhaps you see yourself as so apart from the rest of the world that you actually feel what is the point of meeting with friends who don't know what's bothering you? Having dropped out of things a few times, you may drop out because you don't want to face your friends' reactions. It is obvious that if your friends don't know about your eating disorder, they will get very fed up with you and find your behaviour difficult to understand.

One way to improve the situation might be to tell your friends about your eating problem.

### With a Little Help from My Friends

Friends often are much easier to talk to than parents. Before you tell them, think about what their response might be:

• If your answer is, "they won't want to know, they won't like me if I tell them", you should ask yourself, is this really true? Or is it more likely to be a fear YOU have? If you are pretty certain your friends will not respond positively, maybe you should reconsider whether they are worth your while to be nurtured as friends.

- If the answer is, "they will be sympathetic, but they won't understand", maybe you need to educate them about your problem. You could give them this book, for instance.
- If your answer is, "of course my best friend would not think badly of me because of my eating problem, but still I couldn't tell her. ... " You should think why it is so difficult for you to confide. What do you have to lose? Getting better involves letting go of your problem a bit, letting others in to listen and support. If you need to keep your problem totally secret, perhaps that says something about your motivation to change. Perhaps it isn't quite as strong as you thought.

Perhaps you have told your friends about your eating disorder long ago but you still worry about the effect your eating disorder is having on your relationship with them. You should ask yourself the following:

- Do you make an effort to look after your friendships, or do you always wait for someone else to ring you? Making the first move in a relationship is very frightening. Maybe you feel, "I don't want to be seen to need somebody." Perhaps you fear people will only go out with you out of pity. Remember, we all depend on others. Needing others and admitting you want their company is not weakness, it is actually a strength. How do YOU feel when someone rings YOU up? Is your first thought that they are weak for wanting to be with you? Surely not!

## Making Friends

Perhaps you have already lost some or all of your friends or have gradually grown away from them. If there aren't any old friendships you could rekindle, maybe you need to make a fresh start. Here are a few suggestions that may help you in making the first steps towards meeting new people.

- It is important not to set your sights too high. You will not make very deep friendships within the space of a few weeks. However, you may be able to have regular social contact with people who you feel are quite nice. And that is definitely better than festering alone at home.
- Don't be too choosy. Go out with people, even if you don't think they are going to become your best friend. Firstly, your initial instincts may be proved wrong. And secondly, these people may introduce you to their friends.
- Expect setbacks and rejections. You may find yourself in the position of having to ask a number of people to do something with you before

you get a positive response. This is very disheartening, and you may feel very tempted to think, "nobody likes me". Remember, there are many possible reasons why someone might not be able to go out with you. Most of these reasons will have nothing to do with you. Try to think of examples when you had to turn someone down because you were busy, tired, going out with someone else, having to take the dog to the vet's, or because you had an exam the next day. Most people actually like being asked out, even if they can't make it.

- If you join an evening class to meet people, expect that some classes will not generate much contact outside the actual class. Certain classes will make it much more likely that you get to know others. It is much easier to chat whilst you do pottery than during a maths course.

Below is a list of suggestions of how to meet people. Think of some ideas which you might add to the list.

- evening classes
- sports clubs
- environmental organisations
- pressure groups (Amnesty, Greenpeace)
- church activities
- invite your neighbours over for a drink
- invite work colleagues over

## SEXUAL RELATIONSHIPS

Sexual relationships are a sore point for many people.

Perhaps you have watched your parents in very unhappy or unsuccessful relationships. Perhaps you were sexually abused during your childhood or had frightening or unpleasant sexual encounters as an adult. Maybe this has left you feeling suspicious and wary of sexual relationships, or it has made you feel you are not a worthwhile person, and you therefore continue to plunge yourself into sexual relationships that are unrewarding, destructive, and undermine your self-esteem further. Whatever your particular pattern is, you will need time to think about it and change it.

### Are You Frightened of Sex?

The thought of having a physical relationship may be absolutely terrifying for you. Perhaps this is part of a general fear of getting too close to anyone, or you feel so bad about your body that you can't bear the thought of someone touching you—or maybe you have been brought up in a family where sex was regarded as a taboo, or perhaps you have been abused.

*Kate*

Kate was a 25-year-old teacher who had developed an eating disorder when she was 15. She had never had a boyfriend, which she was very sad about. "I just couldn't handle the thought of anyone getting close to me, but at the same time I felt desperately lonely." All her male friends were gay. She shared a house with one of them. He was her closest friend and helped her a great deal in overcoming her eating disorder. She practically spent all her spare time with him. When her eating disorder improved, she began to recognise that her friendship was safe and rewarding, but also rather limited, and that it stopped her from meeting other people. She was very frightened of moving out, but in the end she decided that this was her only chance to change her situation.

If you are frightened of sexual contact:

- Ask yourself whether, like Kate, you are hiding away without the opportunity to meet someone? If you want to overcome your fear, maybe you need to change your lifestyle.
- If your fear of sex is fear of the unknown, maybe you should take some steps to remedy the deficits in your education. A reading list is given at the end of the chapter.
- If you have a partner, think very hard whether you can let them know how you feel about sex?

## The Wrong Man

Perhaps you repeatedly get into relationships with the wrong partner—someone who initially attracts and excites you, but then things turn sour repeatedly in the same way. Instead of turning from frog into prince, your partners stay frogs no matter how much you kiss them.

It may be that you are searching for someone who displays characteristics you would like to have but may also lack values and attributes you hold and cherish, and so it goes wrong.

*Vanessa*

Vanessa was a very image-conscious young woman, who spent all her money on designer clothes and make-up. "Men see me just as a sexy blonde." All her boyfriends were good-looking muscular types. "Whenever I go to the night club with one of my boyfriends, people will turn round and look at us admiringly. I rather enjoy that, and I think all the preparation beforehand was worth it." All her boyfriends were extremely jealous of other men and whilst initially in a relationship she enjoyed this, later on she would find

Kiss! Kiss!

Still a frog?

Nothing changes

it irritating and claustrophobic. One of her boyfriends beat her up out of jealousy, and another one created a fuss in a night-club and they were banned. "I have often asked myself, why do I always go for the same type of man? I still don't know why. I am just not attracted to someone who isn't good-looking no matter how nice they are."

If you repeatedly get involved with the wrong type of men, ask yourself:

- What is it that attracts you to that kind of man?
- What does your choice say about you?
- Are you drawn to people who display features that you are lacking?

Changing your pattern may be difficult. Remember, the first step towards change is recognising and accepting that there is a problem.

## Promiscuity

To go through a phase of short-lived sexual relationships in a trial-and-error fashion is perhaps not that uncommon for many young people. However, this pattern can become a problem.

### Deirdre

Deirdre is a 26-year-old nurse. She has never had a steady boyfriend. Since her teens she has had many brief relationships, none of them lasting for longer than a few weeks. She has also had quite a few one-night stands. "I find it very easy to start relationships, and initially I am very keen on whoever I am with. But that seems to change quite quickly, and I get very bored, and I then have to get rid of them very quickly. A few times I have had a one-night stand when I have drunk too much, and that's at times been quite unpleasant."

### Yvonne

Yvonne is 30. Her father, whom she has never met, was from Jamaica; her mother, who was Scottish, was an alcoholic. Yvonne grew up in a children's home, where she was bullied. When she was 12 she was raped by some older boys. She was too scared to tell anyone. She became a prostitute when she was 17. She is now unemployed and lives on her own with her two children. She has never used contraception. She has been pregnant 12 times altogether. She had 5 miscarriages and 5 abortions.

If you are changing your partners more quickly than Casanova, ask yourself why you are doing it:

- Do you get a kick out it? Does it feel like something slightly forbidden, slightly dangerous? If that's the case, what other sources of excitement do you have in your life?
- Sometimes promiscuity is the result of extremely low self-esteem. Do you plunge yourself into relationships because you feel you somehow don't deserve any better? Or to make yourself feel better? In the long run this is going to make you feel worse about yourself.
- Are you usually drunk when you get sexually involved? Why do you let yourself?
- Do you use sex as a way of pleasing others? Is it the only way you know of gaining acceptance (love)?

Whatever your reasons for promiscuity are:

- Make sure you protect yourself against pregnancy and sexually transmitted disease.

## CHILDREN

Periods usually stop in anorexia nervosa as a direct result of starvation. Many women with eating disorders worry therefore, about whether they will be able to have babies, what a pregnancy would be like for them, and whether they might damage their unborn baby. We have tried to answer some of the most commonly asked questions in this area.

### Will I Be Able to Get Pregnant?

Very little is known about the fertility of women with anorexia nervosa after they have gained weight. What is known, though, is that some women get pregnant despite very irregular or even absent periods, even though their eating disorder is still active.

### Could I Have Damaged My Baby?

- If, by the time you get pregnant, you have overcome your eating disorder and you are at a healthy weight and eating normally, there is nothing to be worried about.
- If you starve yourself regularly during pregnancy, your baby is at risk of being born prematurely and underweight. Both these factors will make the baby more susceptible to illness. We don't know what effects repeated vomiting or abuse of laxatives have on the unborn child.

### What Will Happen to My Eating Disorder during Pregnancy?

Many women with eating disorders who get pregnant manage to get their symptoms under control during pregnancy because their wish not to harm their baby is very strong. After the baby is born, many go back to their old habits. So, if you are planning to get pregnant, it is definitely best to try to sort your eating disorder out first.

*Rosie*

Rosie used approximately 100 laxative tablets every time she binged. The after-effects of this were terrible for her—she suffered severe pain and massive diarrhoea. During a short-lived relationship with a man she got pregnant and decided to keep the baby. "As soon as I knew I was pregnant, I knew that I had to stop taking my laxatives. Once during pregnancy when I over-ate, I took some laxatives on the spur of the moment, without thinking about it. Afterwards I got so worried about having damaged my baby that for the rest of my pregnancy I didn't touch the stuff at all. Now I have got a beautiful baby boy of 6 months. He has transformed my life. I am still breast-feeding a little, so I am still not taking any laxatives, but I know that when he is not going to be dependent on me physically any more I might easily fall back."

## Will I Cope with Putting on Weight during Pregnancy?

The prospect of weight gain during pregnancy can be daunting— whether or not you suffer from an eating disorder. Many women worry about whether they will be able to return to their previous shape after pregnancy. In our experience, eating-disordered mothers have similarly varied responses to the weight and shape changes of pregnancy as non-eating-disordered mothers. Some cope well, others feel huge.

## I Am Worried about Being a Bad Mother

Many women with eating disorders are very good mothers. It must be said, however, that the stresses of handling an eating problem and raising a child sometimes do take their toll. Some bulimic mothers may find it very difficult to feed their children because they are stuck between the extreme poles of total control or no control.

*Wendy*

Wendy was a single mother of a 7-year-old daughter. Her bulimia had started before her child's birth. "I have never been able to eat with her, which I find incredibly sad. She only has me, and really we should eat together. But I simply find it too difficult. I serve her tea and then busy myself with something else. When she has finished, I quickly throw the leftovers away. She used to accept my behaviour unquestioningly, but now that she is older, of course she wants to know why I never sit down with her. The other day she told me how nice it had been when she visited a friend's house where the whole family had sat down together for their tea.

Another problem is, we are quite hard up, and I often say to her, you can't have this or that because we have no money. It makes me feel terrible to have to deny her things just because I waste so much money on my binges."

Others find it difficult to get the correct balance of discipline that every child needs.

*Ellie*

Ellie had a boy aged 9 and a girl aged 5. She had little support from her husband in bringing up the children as he was a long-distance lorry driver and often away from home for long stretches of time. "Both my children are quite difficult, especially Oliver, my 9-year-old, who is quite a handful. When I am in one of my bingeing phases, I have no time or energy to do anything with them other than the absolute basics. I let them watch the TV for hours whilst I am in the kitchen stuffing myself. During these phases I don't manage to be firm with them, and both of them tend to play up much more then. At other times, when I am not bingeing, I try to make up to them—I read with them, take them to the park, or invite some of their friends round to play. I also don't let them get away with it if they are naughty. But I somehow fear my inconsistent handling is going to damage them. In fact, Oliver's school said he was quite badly behaved, and we will have to go and see a child psychologist."

If you have children and are worried about the effect of your eating disorder on them, ask yourself the following questions:

- Are you right to be worried? What is the evidence for your worry? Are you trying to be "a good-enough mother" or are you trying to be a perfect mother? Is it possible that the thinking traps outlined in chapter 10 might trip you up in the area of mothering, too?

If, on close questioning, you decide that, well, basically you are doing fine, other people seem to think your children are delightful and they are thriving, you need read no further.

If you remain worried, what are you worried about? Their diet, their behaviour, their emotional development?

- Use the problem solving approach outlined in chapter 2 to define the problem and think of solutions.

If you are worried about your children's diet, bear in mind the following:

- Don't try to restrict their diet. Children are amazingly good at knowing how much they need.
- Don't ban sweets totally in an attempt to protect your children from an eating disorder. The more you create an aura of forbidden food, the more interested they will become in sweets.
- Try to persuade them to eat some fruit and vegetable every day, but don't panic if your child doesn't share your predilection for health foods.

If you find that you alone or you and your partner can't deal with the worries and difficulties you have with the children, go and get some advice. Don't be ashamed to do so! It can save yourself and your children a lot of misery. Do you have good friends with children? Can you talk to them about your worries? Or maybe your doctor can help or your health visitor.

## FURTHER READING

Amodeo, J., & Wentworth, K. (1986). *A guide to successful relationships*. London: Arkana.

Beck, A.T. (1988). *Love is never enough. How couples can overcome conflicts and solve relationship problems through cognitive therapy*. London: Penguin Books.

Byrne, K. (1987). *The parent's guide to anorexia and bulimia*. New York: Schocken Books.

Comfort, A. (1982). *The joy of love*. London: Quartet Books.

Dickson, A. (1985). *The mirror within*. London: Quartet Books.

Friday, N. (1986). *My secret garden*. London: Quartet Books.

Norwood, R. (1986). *Women who love too much! When You keep wishing and hoping he'll change*. London: Arrow Books.

Skynner, R., & Cleese, J.  (1983). *Families and how to survive them*. London: Methuen.

CHAPTER FOURTEEN

# Working to Live, Living to Work

Having a regular day-time occupation, whether it is paid work, house-work, studying, or voluntary work, is an important part of our lives. If it's the right job for the right person, work can be an important source of self-esteem. It can provide pleasure, challenge, and stimulation. Very few people actually feel that positively about their job at all times, but they still appreciate the fact that their work gives them independence, a sense of purpose, and a daily routine.

Many sufferers of eating disorders have difficulties with their work. Such problems can have very different sources. They may simply be the result of difficult work conditions like a nasty boss, long working hours, shiftwork, low pay, or sexual harassment. Sometimes sufferers of bulimia—because they feel bad about themselves or because they are frightened of change—get into, and stay in, bad jobs. Problems at work can also arise as a result of a mismatch between the job and the person doing it.

## SOME COMMON WORK PROBLEMS

### I Don't Have a Job

Whilst there are many reasons for being out of work, some people lose their job as a result of their eating disorder.

*Hazel*

Hazel was 19. She had wanted to be a nurse all her life. She was overjoyed when she got into a nursing course at a major teaching hospital. However, she dropped out of it within a few weeks "as it didn't seem like what I had imagined it at all". Her parents were very critical of her decision and felt she should not have given up so quickly. In order to earn some money, she began to work in a restaurant. "I had to give that up, too, as I just couldn't cope with all the food around. The owner began to notice that bits were missing." She then took up a job in a trendy boutique as a shop assistant. "Everybody there was very slim and figure-conscious. I found that very difficult, especially if I had a binge the night before. I just couldn't face going in feeling all fat and horrible. So in the end I lost the job." She spent two months at home with her eating disorder getting worse, and with constant criticisms from her mother. Although she'd routinely go to the job centre, she never actually went to any job interviews. "I had totally lost my confidence."

If you are out of a job and frightened of starting again, you should think about the following:

- Being out of work is bound to make your eating disorder worse due to lack of structure and boredom.
- Perhaps your eating disorder is so severe that you feel you can't hold down a full-time job. You may be right. Maybe you should think of doing a part-time job or voluntary work, just to get you going and to build up your confidence.
- Perhaps you are telling yourself that you are just waiting for the right job to come along. Whilst there is certainly something to be said for trying to find the right job, you should try to be honest with yourself and ask yourself whether the right job is likely to come along. Maybe you are just avoiding making a start.
- If you are frightened of going to job interviews, is there anyone who could help you with this problem? It may be very useful to role-play such a situation. If there isn't anyone who you trust enough to do this with you, write down a list of things you may be asked in a job interview. Think in particular about how you are going to explain periods of being out of work. Prepare an answer to each question, and rehearse them aloud to yourself. Do this a few times so you sound fluent and convincing. The better you prepare yourself, the more likely you are going to be successful.

## I Am Not in the Right Job

A lot of misery is caused if you perpetually push yourself to do things you are not cut out to do. Many sufferers of eating disorders have punishingly high expectations of what they should achieve in their jobs. These high expectations may be the result of high expectations your parents had, or still have, of you, and in an attempt to please them you may have gone along with them. Or there may be an attempt to compete with a brother or sister who has done well.

*Virginia*

Virginia came from a family with very high academic expectations. Her father was a university professor. He and her two older brothers had degrees from Cambridge, and it was expected that she would follow in their footsteps. "It was unthinkable in my family not to go to university." At school Virginia had never been very interested in the academic subjects, and she was very unsure what she wanted to do. "The thought of going to university and spending more time studying horrified me. I wanted to get straight into work and earn some money. I knew I was not cut out to be an academic high-flyer like my brothers. Everybody in my family told me I'd regret it if I didn't make the most of my education." With a great deal of hard work and a lot of pressure from her parents, Virginia eventually got into university and started a law course. "My parents were so proud of me, it was unbelievable. On the surface I was pleased, as everybody in my family told me I was doing the right thing. Underneath it all, I was panic-stricken. I just knew I wasn't cut out to be a lawyer. I thought it was utterly boring." Not surprisingly, Virginia's eating disorder, which had started whilst she was still at school in the run-up to her A-levels, got much worse at university. In the end she dropped out of her course. She then took up a job in a big department store as a trainee buyer. She enjoyed this work and was very good at it. "I am still very cross with my parents for pushing me so hard. I know they only meant well, but they got it all wrong."

On the other hand, holding yourself back and aiming too low will cause you to be resentful, unfulfilled, and bored.

*Kimberley*

Kimberley had worked as a VDU operator in a bank for many years. She was hard-working and reliable. She always got positive feedback from her supervisor in her annual review. Many other people, who had started after her, went for promotion and got it, but she was too frightened to apply as she was worried about making a mess of the interview. She also felt that, due to her bulimia, she might not be able cope with more responsibility. At the same time she resented being overtaken by younger colleagues who didn't have half as much experience as she had. "When I thought about the situation rationally, I knew I could do a better job than they did. The longer the whole situation dragged on, the more resentful I felt about the whole situation."

- Write out for yourself how Kimberley should organise herself to plan for promotion. Use chapter 2 for help.

*Juliette*

Juliette was a bright young woman who had an English degree. As a child she had been her father's favourite, and he had always emphasised the importance of a good career to her. She felt that he was quite disappointed when she studied English instead of law, as he had done. After university, she had a couple of jobs with publishing firms, but she couldn't cope with them due to her eating disorder. She then worked on and off as a temporary secretary. She was very unhappy with this, as she felt the work was boring. She had a vague idea of wanting to work in the media but was too scared to make a go of it. "I felt that if I did try it and I failed, I'd be worse off than ever. I also knew that everybody in my family would be extremely sceptical if I tried yet another new career and that I would be unable to cope with that. I often looked at job adverts and considered applying, but then I'd get too panic-stricken. I felt trapped by my indecision." Juliette came into therapy for her eating disorder. She began to realise that she might easily go on wasting much more time being a temp and that it was unrealistic that she'd be given a dream job in the media in view of her work record. She decided to apply for a permanent secretarial post within a television company, as this would allow her to take a good look at a field of work in which she was interested and help her decide whether she really wanted to get deeper into it.

- Imagine you were Juliette using problem solving techniques (chapter 2) to draw up a decision making sheet.

## Workaholics

Some people spend practically all their waking hours working. Very few of them actually enjoy this. If you are one of those few, you need read no further. Most workaholics, however, overwork out of a sense of battling against personal failure or out of perfectionism ("If I don't give my everything ... I might as well not bother ... people will think I am no good.") Re-read chapter 10 and try to work out where your striving for success and perfectionism comes from. Overwork takes it's toll by making an eating disorder worse.

*Sylvia*

Sylvia was a trainee accountant. She worked in a firm where it was simply expected that employees worked for 10 to 12 hours a day. Often she'd have to go in at week-ends to be able to meet deadlines. She was also working for her accountancy exams. She never had any breaks at work. When she finally came home in the evening, she needed several glasses of whisky to wind down, and then she'd have a binge. She often felt that she couldn't go on like this for much longer. She found it very difficult to come for treatment, as it interfered with her punishing schedule. It took Sylvia a long time to realise that she had a part to play in creating some of the pressures at work for herself. It turned out that she worked harder than any of her colleagues. As she never had any breaks, she was often overtired and therefore inefficient and slow. Sylvia was asked to allow herself to have three breaks in the day and to eat something each time she had a break. "It was very difficult for me to do this. I had to tell myself over and over again that I wouldn't get better without it. There were always temptations to get out of having a break." Once Sylvia had got into a routine of having breaks, she managed to work much more efficiently and actually began to enjoy her job again. Her evening binges gradually lessened.

Sometimes overworking can be the result of an exaggerated sense of duty or responsibility.

*Eleni*

Eleni was the oldest daughter of a Greek Cypriot family. For many years her parents had worked extremely hard to build up a small restaurant. "They always said they did it so that my sisters and me would have it better than them one day." Eleni worked as a nurse and lived at home. She felt to show her gratitude she ought to help her parents, so all her spare time and at week-ends she waitressed in her parents' restaurant. When she occasionally had an evening to herself she was much too tired to go out and instead binged. Her younger sisters helped out much less. The middle sister was a student and claimed she was far too busy to help, and the youngest one had left home and was living with an English boyfriend. "My sisters are really rather selfish. My parents complain about them to me, but at the end of the day they do let them get away with it, and all the helping falls back on me." Eleni felt that she couldn't go her own way, as this would be like betraying her parents.

If you habitually overwork, you have a problem with balancing your "shoulds" and "wants". Go to chapter 8 and re-read the section on life style balance.

## Is Your Job Right for You?

If you are unhappy with your job, go through the list below and write down all the positive and negative aspects of your job in the same way as you constructed your bulimia balance sheet in chapter 1. It is also worth asking yourself where you want to be in five years' time.

Let's consider Susan's case.

*Susan*

After leaving school with her A levels, Susan started in a bank on a career training course. Her eating disorder developed during this time, and she became increasingly unhappy. This is her balance sheet in which she considered the options in staying in banking.

1. *Gains and Losses for Myself*
   a. *Positive:* The income is good, and I can get a cheap mortgage.
   b. *Negative:* The work is easy but repetitive and not challenging.
   c. *Negative:* I'm given no freedom or chance to take initiative. School was better than this.
   d. *Positive:* If I stay on, I have a chance of promotion.
   e. *Negative:* With increasing computerisation and world financial changes, opportunities may be limited. Another trainee was rejected during her assessment period.
   f. *Negative:* I spend three hours commuting on overcrowded public transport. I have had to drop out of the local dramatic society and do not have time to go to my St. John Ambulance meetings.
2. *Gains and Losses for Others*
   a. *Positive:* My parents welcome the help with the rent that I can give.
   b. *Positive:* My father likes to tell his friends that I work in the city.
   c. *Negative:* I no longer have time to help in the garden or with our pets.
3. *Self-approval or Disapproval*
   a. *Negative:* I don't like the idea that some of our profits come from lending money to poor countries with questionable leaders.
   b. *Negative:* I resent the fact that all my work is so materialistic—all for profit.

c. *Negative:* I don't use any of the skills I know I have in dealing with people.

d. *Negative:* I can't use any imagination or flair.

e. *Positive:* I would have the opportunity to return to my job if I have children, and the bank would make part-time work available.

4. *Approval or Disapproval from Others*

a. *Positive:* My parents are proud of me working in the city.

b. *Negative:* My friends in the drama society are rather disparaging about my boring city job.

c. *Negative:* I hate it that we are the butt of so much public anger. You constantly have to face customers who are angry that the cash dispenser has gone wrong or that their statement is inaccurate or that they have had to wait too long in the queue.

If there are more stresses, difficulties and minuses than positive things about your job, perhaps it is time to change. Why don't you sit down for a brainstorming session to sort this out.

To make an effective decision about your job, apply the decision making steps used earlier in chapter 2.

*Step 1:* Define the problem with your current job clearly and concretely.

*Step 2:* Write down any alternative jobs that you half think you would like to do. This brainstorming requires you to produce ideas without censorship (ignore the voice that says that your father would not approve or that you are bound to fail). Imaginative, wild, and even ridiculous solutions should be included. Quantity rather than quality is important. Later you may need to combine and work on some of these initial ideas.

*Step 3:* Write down the pros and cons of all the alternative solutions you have produced. For some of the options you have come up with you may need to do some research to find out what is actually involved in a particular job.

*Step 4:* Rank the available options in terms of your priorities.

You should now be a lot clearer about what you want and what is realistic for you.

## FURTHER READING

Back, K., & Back. K. (1982). Assertiveness at work. New York: McGraw Hill.

Edelmann, R.J. *Interpersonal conflicts at work.* Leicester: BPS Books.

Fontana, D. (1993). *Managing time.* Leicester: BPS Books.

Fontana, D. (1990). *Social skills at work.* Leicester: BPS Books.

CHAPTER FIFTEEN

# Is this the End of the Journey—Or Not?

Having worked through this book, ask yourself honestly how you feel. If it has helped you and you are a good step further on your journey towards recovery, excellent! Enjoy the feeling of rest after some hard work. But be prepared for further obstacles along the way. But then, getting better is not about being free of problems—rather, it is about feeling better equipped to deal with them, about feeling more courageous and prepared to try out new things, to look at problems afresh, not to be so trapped by the harsh routines of dieting, the chaos of binges, and the efforts constantly to please others.

## BUT WHAT IF YOU ARE STILL STUCK?
If you feel nothing has changed and nothing will ever change, have you actually allowed yourself to work through this book properly? Or have you just rushed through it in a "bingey" sort of fashion and then declared it useless? Maybe you do need to slow down a bit and need to go over it again chapter by chapter. That may seem boring, irritating, tedious, and too difficult to do. Did you know that the people who are most successful in life are the ones who don't give up when they encounter failure? So try again.

## DREAM ON, BABY
You may say, "I can't identify with the stories of the women in the book. My problems are different. I can't do anything to change them. Only someone very special can sort them out." It is possible that you are right

and that you do need specialist help. But perhaps—and only you can know this—this is just wishful thinking, an excuse, so as to not face the hardships of the journey to recovery.

## The Straw that Broke the Camel's Back

Maybe the reason why you haven't been able to change anything is that there are too many things going on in your life that are stressful and difficult, and it feels like you can't juggle all these balls at once.

Go back to the problem-solving chapter (chapter 2) and think again. What is going on in your life that is taking up so much of your time and energies that you can't concentrate on your needs? Is it something to do with your relationships? Is it to do with work? Studies? Your children? Think about it this way: Builders have to do some groundwork before they can start building a house, like clearing the terrain, getting the materials, etc. Without these preparations their task becomes impossible.

*Patsy*

Patsy was a 50-year-old full-time teacher, who was married with two teenage children. She was also looking after her invalid elderly father in her home. She had to get up several times at night to make sure he was alright and was completely drained by this. She said her husband and children were very supportive. She had in the past also cared devotedly for her mother, until she died three years ago.

She binged several times daily and couldn't understand why this happened. When we gave her this book, she felt that the problems described were not hers. She said that the women in the book were much younger than she, and she felt she had little in common with them. She was very angry about being "lumped in" with people who made themselves sick, which was not one of her problems. In talking to her, it became clear that although her husband and children were sympathetic towards her burden, they actually did very little to help her in practical terms. For example, neither her husband nor her children, who were 13 and 15, did anything in the household. Patsy would go as far as cleaning their shoes and even making sandwiches for everybody to take to school and work. Although Patsy was an extremely bright and well-read woman, she failed to recognise that bingeing was her only way of relieving tension and stress. She had no time for herself and was continuously driven by "shoulds". She experienced reading the book and coming for treatment as further chores and pressures on her, designed to humiliate rather than help her.

If you are a bit like Patsy, try to think of what ground work you have to do, to change your life and allow yourself to concentrate on your eating problem.

## RECOVERY: A TRIP INTO UNCHARTED TERRITORY

If you have had an eating disorder for a very long time and it is a very deeply ingrained pattern, changing your habit may be extremely anxiety-provoking, like a journey into the unknown. Or you may fear that if you change a tiny bit, you will set loose an avalanche of change that you then can't contain. Is there really nothing you can do? Perhaps it would be helpful for you to join a self-help group. Find out what is available locally. Or go and talk to your general practitioner. Take the book with you. Tell him or her that you have tried your best to help yourself, but that you need someone to help you to start the journey to recovery properly.

Whatever your story, whatever your outcome, we would like to hear from you. Tell us how you got on with this book, what you found helpful or not so helpful, how you managed to overcome your eating problem, or what stopped you or is still stopping you from overcoming it. You can write to us directly:

Dr. Ulrike Schmidt and Dr. Janet Treasure
Eating Disorder Unit Maudsley Hospital
Denmark Hill
London SE5 8AZ

# APPENDIX
## Food Diary

| Time | What eaten | B | V | L | Antecedents & Consequences |
|------|------------|---|---|---|----------------------------|
|      |            |   |   |   |                            |

B = Binge,  V = Vomited,  L = Laxatives

# Some Useful Addresses

Alcohol Concern
305 Gray's Inn Road
London WC1X 8QF

AlAnon Family Groups
61 Dover Street
London SE1 4YR
071-403 0888

Alcoholics Anonymous
Head Office
Stonebow House
Stonebow
York YO1 2NJ
0904-644026

British Association for Counselling
37a Sheep Street
Rugby
Warwickshire
W21 3BX
0788-78328/9

Debtors Anonymous
071-328 4802

Eating Disorders Association
Sackville Place
44-48 Magdalen Street
Norwich
Norfolk
0603-621414

National Association of Young People's
Counselling & Advisory Services
17-23 Albion Street
Leicester
LE1 6GD
0533-554775

Relate
Herbert Gray College
Little Church Street
Rugby
Warwickshire
CV21 3AP
0788-73241